*TWAYNE'S WORLD AUTHORS SERIES*
*A Survey of the World's Literature*

Sylvia E. Bowman, Indiana University
GENERAL EDITOR

# GERMANY

Ulrich Weisstein, Indiana University
EDITOR

*Rolf Hochhuth*

TWAS 463

Rolf Hochhuth

# ROLF HOCHHUTH

By MARGARET E. WARD
*Wellesley College*

TWAYNE PUBLISHERS
A DIVISION OF G. K. HALL & CO., BOSTON

**Library of Congress Cataloging in Publication Data**

Ward, Margaret E
    Rolf Hochhuth.

    (Twayne's world authors series ; TWAS 463 :
Germany)
    Bibliography: p. 165–72.
    Includes index.
    1.   Hochhuth, Rolf        —Criticism and inter-
pretation.   I.   Title.
PT2668.03Z94   1977        832'.9'14        77–3452
ISBN  0-8057-6300-7

For Thomas

# Contents

About the Author

Preface

Chronology

1. Introduction: The Search for Truth through History    15

2. *The Deputy:* A Christian Tragedy    25

3. *Soldiers: Obituary for Geneva*    48

4. The Artist and Politics: Letters, Essays, Speeches    71

5. Hochhuth's American Revolution    85

6. The Comedies    100

7. Monologues of Resignation    126

8. Conclusion    139

   Notes and References    147

   Selected Bibliography    165

   Index    173

# About the Author

Margaret E. Ward received the B.A. degree, magna cum laude, from Wilson College in 1965 and the M.A. and Ph.D. in German at Indiana University in 1967 and 1973 respectively. Two years of research in Berlin and Paris provided the basis for her (unpublished) doctoral thesis, "Peter Weiss, Rolf Hochhuth, Armand Gatti: The interaction between intent, content and form in contemporary political drama." In addition to book reviews she is the author of "Armand Gatti, Bertolt Brecht and the Theory of Identification" to be published in *Brechtjahrbuch,* 1977. Dr. Ward, Assistant Professor of German at Wellesley College, Wellesley Massachusetts, was awarded an Early Leave in 1976-77, which provided the opportunity for further research in the field of contemporary political drama, including extensive travel in East and West Germany.

# *Preface*

Since the publication in 1964 of *The Storm over The Deputy* (ed. Eric Bentley), which documented the controversy surrounding Rolf Hochhuth's first play, no other book has appeared in English concerning this German author. And despite his considerable contribution to the theater of the 1960s and 1970s in West Germany, the first book length study to appear in the Federal Republic since the 1967 monograph by Siegfried Melchinger in the Friedrich's world dramatists series is that by Rainer Taëni, published as this book goes to print (see bibliography).

*The Deputy* immediately established Hochhuth's world reputation. It had seventy-five different productions in twenty-seven countries and was translated into seventeen languages. Two English translations are available: *The Representative,* trans. Robert David MacDonald (London); and *The Deputy,* trans. Richard and Clara Winston (New York). Hochhuth's second play, *Soldiers,* was translated into ten languages. The English translation by Robert David MacDonald is available in both American and British editions. Thirty-seven productions of the play in eleven countries firmly established Hochhuth as a dramatist of international stature.

Although Hochhuth has continued to write prolifically, little else is available to speakers of English who are interested in his controversial contribution to the political and literary discussions of the last decade in Germany. Translations of his essays are entirely lacking, and his four major plays since 1968: *Guerillas, Die Hebamme, Lysistrate und die Nato,* and *Tod eines Jägers* have not been rendered into English, despite the fact that the first has the United States as its setting and the last deals with the American author Ernest Hemingway.

In the secondary literature in both English and German, Hochhuth has invariably been treated in the general context of the "documentary drama" of the 1960s. This monograph, in addition to providing the first general introduction to his *oeuvre* in English, also tries to correct the somewhat distorted impression that has thus been created. It will show the close correlation between Hochhuth's developing *Weltanschauung* and his approach to dramaturgy. Chapter 1 introduces the literary, philosophical, and political background that is a prerequisite for understanding Hochhuth's early dramatic practice. The fourth chapter continues this discussion of the playwright's world view by analyzing his political essays, falling slightly out of the otherwise chronological sequence. Since Hochhuth has made his mark in German and world literature as a dramatist and essayist, analysis of his minor prose and of his poetry has been excluded except where it is directly relevant to one of the dramas.

Wherever possible, quotations are given in English from existing translations. In all other cases, the author takes full responsibility for translations from the German. Where a passage presents unusual syntax or play on words, the original has been given in a footnote. In the case of Hochhuth's works, abbreviations have been used in the text as follows: De for *The Deputy* (New York, 1964); Dr for *Dramen* (Reinbek, 1972); G for *Guerillas* (Reinbek, 1970); H for *Die Hebamme* (Reinbek, 1971); K for *Krieg und Klassenkrieg* (Reinbek, 1971); L for *Lysistrate und die Nato* (Reinbek, 1973); S for *Soldiers* (New York, 1968); So for *Soldaten* (Reinbek, 1967); St for *Der Stellvertreter* (Reinbek, 1963); T for *Tod eines Jägers* (Reinbek, 1976); and Z for *Zwischenspiel in Baden-Baden* (Reinbek, 1974).

I am indebted to Ulrich Weisstein for his encouragement in undertaking this monograph and to Wellesley College for granting an Early Leave during which the project was completed. Thanks also go to Thomas de Witt, whose critical comments as historian and advice and support as husband were invaluable.

MARGARET E. WARD

*Wellesley, Massachusetts*

# Chronology

1931    Born in Eschwege on the Werra (now in West Germany).

1941    Member of *Deutsches Jungvolk,* the junior branch of the Hitler youth.

1945    American occupation of Eschwege. Hochhuth acts as a messenger for his uncle, appointed mayor by the occupation forces.

1948    Leaves school before completing *Abitur* (high school diploma). Works as a bookseller in Eschwege, Marburg, Heidelberg, and Munich.

1950-    Early prose attempts:"Inventur"; *Victoriastrasse Nr. 4.*

1955    Editor for the Bertelsmann Verlag in Gütersloh; works on a Wilhelm Busch reader.

1957    Marries Marianne Heinemann, whom he has known since his school years.

1959    Goes to Rome to write first draft of *Der Stellvertreter.* Writes "Resignation oder die Geschichte einer Ehe" (story).

1961    Writes *Die Berliner Antigone* (novella). Editor of *Liebe in unserer Zeit: 32 Erzählungen.*

1962    Receives *Gerhart Hauptmann-Förderungspreis.* Editor of a commemorative edition of Theodor Storm's collected works, *Am grauen Meer.*

1963    February 20: premiere of *Der Stellvertreter* under the direction of Erwin Piscator at the Freie Volksbühne in West Berlin. Drama published the same day by Rowohlt. Awarded Berlin's *Junge Generation* literary prize.

1963    Answer to *Theater heute* questionnaire: "Soll das Theater die heutige Welt darstellen?" Moves with his family to Basle, Switzerland.

1964    Receives Frederic Melcher Award during visit to U.S.A. Sends letter to the President of the Federal Republic, Heinrich Lübke, concerning limitation of air warfare through the Red Cross.

1965    "Der Klassenkampf ist nicht zu Ende" (essay) appears in *Der Spiegel.*

1966    Death of Piscator; Hochhuth writes *Nekrolog* (obituary).

1967 October 9: premiere of *Soldaten* at the Freie Volksbühne, Hans Schweikart, director. Drama published simultaneously. Prohibition of *Soldiers* at London's National Theater.

1968 May 28: speech against the *Notstandsgesetze* (emergency laws), "Die Sprache der Sozialdemokraten." "Hat die Revolution in der Bundesrepublik eine Chance?" published in *Der Spiegel*. "Angst vor der 'Schutz'-Macht USA" (essay) published in *konkret*. Writes "L'Impromptu de Madame Tussaud" (story).

1970 March 20: speech against the Vietnam War, "Appell an Verteidigungsminister Schmidt." "Unsere 'abgeschriebenen' Schriftsteller in der Bundesrepublik," an appeal on behalf of older writers. April: publication of *Guerillas,* his third drama. May: premiere of *Guerillas* in Stuttgart (Württembergisches Staatstheater), with Peter Palitzsch as director.

1971 Publication of the comedy *Die Hebamme,* along with a collection of stories and poems, as well as essays, including "Der alte Mythos vom 'neuen' Menschen: Vorstudie zu einer Ethologie der Geschichte." Publication of *Krieg und Klassenkrieg,* a collection of essays, including the defense of *Guerillas,* "Keine Revolution ohne Infiltration." March 6: open letter to Chancellor Willy Brandt concerning the homeless in the Federal Republic.

1972 Publication of *Dramen,* including *Der Stellvertreter, Soldaten,* and *Guerillas* with commentaries. May: simultaneous premiere of *Die Hebamme* in theaters in Munich, Essen, Göttingen and Zurich. Hochhuth divorced.

1973 Publication of *Lysistrate und die Nato,* a comedy, along with a study, "Frauen und Mütter, Bachofen und Germaine Greer." Editor of *Kaisers Zeiten,* a volume of photographs from the archives of the court photographers O. and G. Tellgmann.

1974 February 22: simultaneous premiere of *Lysistrate und die Nato* at the Wiener Volkstheater, directed by Peter Lotschak, and in Essen under the direction of Erich Schumacher. *Zwischenspiel in Baden-Baden* published, an expanded version of "Resignation oder die Geschichte einer Ehe."

1976   Publication of *Tod eines Jägers,* a monodrama about the suicide of Ernest Hemingway. Winter semester: lectures at Essen University on theory of political theater. December 2: awarded the Basle Art Prize.

CHAPTER 1

# Introduction: The Search for Truth through History

## I  *Boyhood in Wartime*

R OLF Hochhuth has said, " 'Authors must articulate the bad conscience of their nation because politicians have such a good one.'"[1] It is clear from this statement that he envisions himself as an engaged author, as the self-appointed articulator for a nation with a bad conscience. Yet over the years he has remained reticent about any personal experiences during the formative years that might have led him to embark on this political literary mission at the age of thirty.

In a rare exception, an interview in 1964 with the art editor of the *San Francisco Chronicle* (published originally in *Ramparts*), Hochhuth told of his boyhood in Eschwege on the Werra River, where he was born in 1931. His father, director of a shoe factory that had been in the family for three generations, had retired as an army officer after serving only a few months in World War II. The young Hochhuth's wartime experiences were, according to this account, typical for a boy of his age. His parents listened clandestinely to the American and British broadcasts and extended a welcome to the Jewish wife of a cousin, who lived with them for several weeks in 1943 before taking her own life.[2] But Rolf, whose brother was on the Eastern front, feared the Russians, hated the English for their bombing of the nearby city of Kassel, and hoped that Germany would win: " 'To the end of the war, the little boy Rolf wished that Germany would win. My parents did not wish it, and they would never have thought it possible that Germany could win after the invasion of Russia, but, of course, they could not tell their feelings or they would have been killed.'"[3]

15

At age ten Rolf joined the junior division of the Hitler Youth. He had to pick up pamphlets that had been dropped from the air by the Allies, and he scorned the propaganda contained in them. His unsophisticated opposition to the air war in those days provided the kernel of truth that would later bear fruit in his drama *Soldaten.*

The introspective youth's political and moral concerns were shaped more fully by the events of the early postwar years, however. The Americans occupied Eschwege in 1945, and later the "Iron Curtain" was lowered just four miles from his home, making him keenly aware of the problem of Germany's division. During these early postwar years, Hochhuth acted as messenger for his uncle, who had been appointed mayor of the town by the Allied military command because he had not been a Nazi. This was also the period when the full horror of the concentration camps was revealed to the German people: "'The photographs were shown in the papers and it shamed and sickened us. We didn't dare to believe. . . .'"[4] And yet one had to believe and contemplate the question of guilt, both national and personal, as Hochhuth did.

Hochhuth decided to leave school at the age of seventeen, before he had completed his *Abitur* (high school diploma). He began to work as a bookseller, first in his home town, and subsequently in Marburg, Heidelberg, and Munich. He himself read prolifically, thus making up in large measure for a lack of formal higher education. Later, after a period of illness which left part of his face paralyzed, he took advantage of his inability to work by attending lectures in philosophy and history at the universities of Heidelberg and Munich. Thus he began his own personal search for truth and for a way to deal with the problem of guilt. This search eventually led him to assume the role of engaged writer, but first he had to discover his literary talent.

## II   *The Literary Beginnings*

During the 1950s Hochhuth not only read a great deal but also began to write. At first he experimented with the lyric genre, then he tried his hand at several short stories and an epistolary novel *(Briefroman)* dealing with the occupation. Most of these early poems and prose works were never published, but Hochhuth included a few in the collection that bears the title of his first comedy, *Die Hebamme,* in 1971.[5] Thomas Mann is the author whom he mentions most often as having influenced him. He identified strongly with Mann's novel *Buddenbrooks,* because his mother's family bore a certain resemblance to the family depicted there. His own attempt at writing a novel, *Victoriastrasse Nr. 4* (referring to the address of his parent's home in Eschwege), was clearly autobiographical. More importantly, however, Hochhuth claims to have been influenced by Mann's whole attitude toward life, "'his humanity, his engagement in politics. I have learned that the poet always must be active in politics. That he is also responsible. *The Deputy* is politics.'"[6]

Hochhuth was surely not referring to the author of the *Betrachtungen eines Unpolitischen (Reflections of an Unpolitical Man),* but rather to the Thomas Mann whom he admired for having left Germany because of his opposition to Hitler. In addition to Thomas Mann, Hochhuth named two other novelists among the literary influences on his work; Robert Musil, and the lesser known Otto Flake, for whom he wrote a moving obituary in 1963 (H, 443-54). Yet such strictly personal admissions of influence are not very fruitful for the literary critic, especially since they refer to novelists, whereas Hochhuth has made his mark in German literature as a dramatist.

A more revealing indicator of Hochhuth's basic literary, philosophical, and political position, which served as a basis for the writing of *The Deputy,* is his answer to a questionnaire in *Theater heute* in 1963, "Soll das Theater die heutige Welt darstellen?" ("Should the theater present today's world?"). This statement shows clearly how his view of history shaped his view of the drama from the very beginning of his literary development (H, 317-26).

### III  *Drama and History*

In his answer Hochhuth affirmed that the theater can and should present today's world, but he immediately limited that portrayal to man as an individual tragic hero. Hochhuth's basic belief in the individual's freedom of choice led him to an aesthetic modeled on Schiller, in direct contrast to the views of Friedrich Dürrenmatt, who, in his essay, *Theaterprobleme,* rejected the idea that it is still possible to have tragic heroes in drama: "Hitler and Stalin cannot be made into Wallensteins."[7] Hochhuth did not specifically mention Dürrenmatt in his answer to the questionnaire, but he surely

had the Swiss dramatist in mind, as is indicated in an interview with
Martin Esslin in 1967: "I don't agree with dramatists like Dürrenmatt who proclaim the end of tragedy on the grounds that the day
of the individual is past forever, that nobody can do anything, that
nobody is responsible any more."[8]

Hochhuth thus pictured himself in the *Theater heute* questionnaire as the champion of the individual, a philosophic as well as
literary cause, in opposition to those who preached that the individual is no longer a meaningful entity in the atomic age. He specifically attacked the sociologist, philosopher, and literary critic
Theodor W. Adorno by quoting him whenever he referred to this
"fashionable" view, and the controversy was continued when
Adorno replied after the first reprinting of the essay in a *Festschrift*
for Georg Lukács in 1966. Hochhuth disagreed with Adorno's
thesis that, in view of the horror of anonymity that characterizes
our modern industrial society, any drama that tries to deal with
reality by portraying it by means of characters and actions is a dis-
grace and sadly distorts that reality. Adorno also noted the danger
inherent in such a dramatic technique — that it would arouse admiration for those who decide whether the button should be pushed
(H, 318).

In a direct rebuttal, Hochhuth maintained that every human
being, even if he suffers an anonymous death in a gas chamber or
as a victim of an atomic bomb, dies as an individual, and that there
remain certain prominent individuals who do face tragic conflicts,
do make significant choices, do shape history, and are therefore
appropriate subjects for the drama. Hochhuth made a strong case
here for the fact that tragedy is still a human, and therefore a literary, possibility: "That is after all the essential task of drama: to insist that man is a responsible being. Or didn't Truman have any responsibility for the destruction of Hiroshima?" (H, 319).

It is apparent that Hochhuth's engagement at this early stage was
basically on behalf of a concept of the drama that would allow for
the individual tragic hero, without any specific political goals: "A
drama that recognizes the human being as an individual does not
need any other engagement beyond this recognition. With that it already achieves more than the current fashion would allow" (H,
320). It is significant that he immediately linked his concept of the
drama as tragedy to his *Weltanschauung* and revealed his dependence on Schiller, calling the German classical dramatist's *Disti-*

*chon:* "'Ehret ihr immer das Ganze, ich kann nur einzelne achten/ Immer im einzelnen nur hab ich das Ganze erblickt'" ("You honor always the whole/ I can only respect the individual. For only through the individual have I perceived the whole") (H, 318) an "eternally true aesthetic law."

Like Schiller, Hochhuth felt that for a humanist the only way to attain the truth was by means of a "personalization" of the conflict of ideas in human history.[9] In fact, without this kind of personalization there could be no drama at all: "It is only humane not to separate the general from the personal; drama leads people into decisions, for where man can no longer decide, there is no drama at all" (H, 318). Hochhuth was willing to admit that the victims of the concentration camps had had little freedom of choice, but "the number of individuals who *did* achieve something has always been very small, throughout history."[10] Yet Hochhuth insisted that although there are only a few prominent individuals who possess "die volle Freiheit der Entscheidung" ("complete freedom of decision"), there is — in principle at least — a certain amount of "Freiheit des Subjekts" ("freedom of the subject") in every human (H, 320). All uniforms, he felt, stop at the collar: "Uniformen haben am Hals ihre Grenze" (H, 320).

The second question posed, "Ist die heutige Welt auf dem Theater überhaupt darstellbar?" ("Can today's world actually be presented in the theater?"), Hochhuth likewise answered in the affirmative, while admitting that there are some limitations. The theater, he felt, was restricted entirely to the human sphere, which explained the impossibility of adequately portraying technology on the stage. He had himself recognized the limit imposed by the inhumane sphere when he tried to represent Auschwitz in *The Deputy*. Once again he relied on Schiller for a comparison, noting the latter's frustration in trying to portray the army of Wallenstein in adequate dramatic terms (H, 321). Hochhuth also admitted that certain themes, like love, are better suited to the epic genre.

## IV     *The Problem of Realism*

The third question asked by *Theater heute* dealt with the important problem of form. "Ist die heutige Welt noch oder wieder mit realistischen Mitteln darstellbar?" ("Can the world of today still, or again, be portrayed with realistic means?") (H, 321). Once again

Hochhuth answered affirmatively, but he qualified his answer with a detailed explanation of what he considered to be "Realism." First he defined it as "the most exact portrayal of the inner and outer situation of man which is imaginable" (H, 321). Yet he conceded that the problem of definition really lies in deciding where Realism begins and ends. Unlike the Marxist critic, Georg Lukàcs, however, who had attempted to set the limits of Realism by means of ideology, eliminating Naturalism on the one hand, and Formalism on the other, Hochhuth took a strictly nonpartisan approach. For him ideology is "die Pest des Zeitalters" ("the plague of the century") (K, 102).

Hochhuth began his discussion of Realism with the question of content, suggesting that dreams and death have more reality for us than much of our daily experience. He then shifted abruptly to the question of form, warning against the use of Surrealistic or Absurd devices. His answer hardly provides a satisfactory solution to a difficult literary problem, but it once again reveals Hochhuth as a dramatist in opposition. He considered his view of the Realistic drama as a legitimate alternative to the Theater of the Absurd and its practitioners, Ionesco and Beckett, whose plays had become popular in Germany by 1960. Hochhuth linked his opposition to the Absurd theater to his belief that drama should function as a tribunal or moral platform for the author. A play in the Absurd tradition is never censored by politicians, he noted, because its criticism remains undirected (H, 323). He felt that his own "Realistic" approach would be more threatening to those he wished to attack.

The use of Realistic devices in the theater, implying the use of documentary material, was therefore an absolute necessity (*unentbehrlich*) for Hochhuth. It meant studying history and distilling the truth from the rubble heap of documents (*Dokumentenschutt*) (G, 10). Hochhuth recognized that one would thus be open to the criticism that one had simply written *Reportage* (journalism), not drama, but he staunchly defended this approach (H, 323–24). The idea of finding the truth through the study of history provides a key both to Hochhuth's *Weltanschauung* and to his dramatic practice and reveals most clearly his reliance on the idealistic aesthetics of Friedrich Schiller, who, like Hochhuth, was an avid student of history.

In his essay "Über die tragische Kunst," Schiller explains that because tragedy has a poetic purpose, the author, while remaining true to history, must subordinate historical accuracy to the poetic purpose, thus following a principle of "natural truth" or "poetic truth" rather than "historical truth."[11] Hochhuth's concept of "Realism," like Schiller's "poetic truth," is not intended to aim at "historical truth," and yet it has its basis in history and has a certain truth of its own. Hochhuth elaborated on this thesis in the "Historische Streiflichter" ("Historical Sidelights") at the conclusion of *The Deputy.* He emphasized that although the author must be free to create fictional characters and scenes, although he should heighten reality through the use of poetic language, the whole must represent the "truth": "If I submit the following notes on controversial events and testimony, it is to demonstrate that as far as possible I have adhered to the facts. I allowed my imagination free play only to the extent that I had to transform the existing raw material of history into drama. Reality was respected throughout, but much of its slag had to be removed" (De, 287). At the same time, the play cannot be simply a re-creation of a given historical event. It must not be "a giant fresco of the past, but rather something indicative, with characters who behave in a way representative of our actions and feelings."[12] It must have symbolic force (De, 287).

As in the *Theater heute* questionnaire, Hochhuth relied on quotations from Schiller to support his position:

The dramatist "cannot use a single element of reality as he finds it; his work must be idealized in *all* its parts if he is to comprehend reality as a whole." Anyone in this day and age who ignores this precept of Schiller, anyone who does not "openly and honestly declare war on naturalism in art," must capitulate in the face of every newsreel — if only because the latter can present "the raw stuff of the world" far more drastically and completely than the stage. For the stage — Bertolt Brecht with his theory of alienation was not the first to discover this — remains true only if, as Schiller says in *Wallenstein,* "it itself frankly destroys the illusion it creates" (De, 287–88).

This passage from the "Sidelights" is reminiscent of Peter Weiss' later contention in his theoretical essay, "Das Material und die Modelle" ("The Material and the Models"), to the effect that a documentary play is not simply a recreation, but that it is art, and therefore different from either the evening news or a street demonstration.[13] But the difference between Weiss and Hochhuth in their approach to documentary material is the latter's total rejection of ideology and his obvious reliance on Schillerian idealistic aesthetics.

Hochhuth's passing reference to Brecht is deceptive, as are the remarks by Erwin Piscator in the introduction to *Der Stellvertreter,* pointing to Brecht, as well as Schiller, as Hochhuth's models (St, 7-11). Hochhuth was certainly influenced by the aesthetics of Schiller, as our subsequent analysis of the plays will seek to demonstrate, but he flatly denies having been influenced by Brecht. In fact, he claims to have consciously avoided studying him.[14]

The *Theater heute* questionnaire already revealed this anti-Brecht position when Hochhuth criticized Brecht's play *Der aufhaltsame Aufstieg des Arturo Ui* (*The Resistable Rise of Arturo Ui*), along with Charlie Chaplin's film *The Great Dictator,* for not taking its subject seriously enough, for making a mockery of history (H, 324). Hochhuth also rejected the general principle of *Verfremdung* (alienation), which he felt had become nothing more than a *Modewort* (fashionable term) (H, 325). Hochhuth thus used the *Theater heute* article not only to present the philosophical and literary basis for his own theater but also to state his opposition to the current trends in the German theater of the 1960s, the Brechtian tradition on the one hand, and the Theater of the Absurd on the other. He thereby placed himself at the fulcrum of an ongoing debate about the nature and the role of drama in the postwar world.

Ironically however, in the conclusion to his answer to the questionnaire, Hochhuth recognized that there might not be such a great difference between the Realistic theater he was advocating and the Absurd theater which he was rejecting, just as he had suggested, in the passage quoted above, a certain affinity between Schiller and Brecht. History is itself, he maintained, the greatest absurdity (H, 325). It is on this point that Adorno reopened the debate several years later. Thus despite the apparent optimism of Hochhuth's approach to the theater, this early statement also reveals an underlying pessimism.

Although Hochhuth recognized the need for political and social change, he felt that history moves in cyclical patterns, and that the basic nature of man cannot be changed: "Der Mensch ändert sich nicht von Grund auf" ("Man does not change his basic nature") (H, 318). Yet despite this pessimistic view of man, characteristic of

Hochhuth's *Weltanschauung,* he continued to assert the power of the individual: "I am a humanist. In other words, I still maintain a belief in the autonomy of the individual and that the individual can make some impact on the world. I repeat: My belief in the power of the individual is small. But that does not mean that one should not — without, I hope, in any way being a hypocrite — write plays about people who prove the opposite."[15]

In Hochhuth's view, the theater ought to be a forum in which timeless lessons can be taught, much along the lines of Schiller's "moralische Anstalt" ("moral institution").[16] For Hochhuth is interested in what he calls the great "polar situations" or conflict situations in history.[17] He sees these as basically conflicts of ideas, but he feels that the drama can only portray them by showing the men who make decisions. "I am very much of the opinion that the history of World War II would have looked very different if Hitler and Churchill had never been born. And indeed I would subscribe to the notion that it would be the end of drama if one were to take the position that man cannot be held responsible for his fate."[18] One can see that Hochhuth repeatedly linked the concept of the freedom of the individual within the historical process to the very possibility for drama. In turn he related this view to the all-important question of guilt and responsibility that had plagued his youth and that found its first poetic expression in *The Deputy.*

Hochhuth conceived of the engaged author as one who would not avoid this issue, the most crucial one for the German people after 1945. But he was not the first author to deal with it. The Swiss dramatist Max Frisch, likewise a disbeliever in ideology and likewise opposed to the vogue of the Absurd, treated it in his play *Andorra,* first performed in Germany in 1962. But Frisch believed that the author could remain aloof from politics, while being committed to a kind of personal truth in "the attempt to create art which is neither national nor international, but more than that, namely a constantly renewed struggle against abstraction, ideology and its lethal weapons."[19] But with its use of parable, *Andorra* did not elicit the same overwhelming response that greeted Hochhuth's *Stellvertreter* just a year later. Hochhuth had realized that the author could not remain entirely aloof from politics, although he must be free of ideological ties. He had also struck a responsive chord in his audience by returning to a traditional Realistic form of drama in approaching the subject of guilt and responsibility.

Subsequently, in talking about life as a tragic Sisyphus game, Hochhuth suggested that the writer must participate quite literally in the struggle for freedom: "Wer schreibt, sollte mitwälzen an dem Stein. Regierende, bekanntlich tun es selten, absolut Regierende niemals" ("Whoever writes should help to heave the stone. Those who govern, as is well known, do it seldom, absolute rulers never") (K, 95). Thus it is left to the writer to articulate the bad conscience of his country and of the world, because those who govern have such a good one. It was in this sense that Hochhuth began work on a drama which in its choice of Pope Pius XII as a central figure was to rock the world and precipitate just the kind of discussion Hochhuth, with his unique sense of moral outrage and engagement, had hoped for. Thus began his mission to reveal to the world the truth of history, as he saw it, through the medium of drama.

## CHAPTER 2

# The Deputy: *A Christian Tragedy*

## I  *Preparation, Publication, Production: Hochhuth, Rowohlt, Piscator*

THE embryo for *The Deputy* were notes that Hochhuth made about the historical figure of Kurt Gerstein, a member of the Protestant Confessing Church, who joined the SS in order to resist Hitler. Placed in a position that gave him firsthand knowledge of what was happening at Auschwitz and Treblinka, he tried, without success, to report these specifics to high church officials in Berlin, in hopes that they might take more direct action (De, 289–95). At first Hochhuth had planned to write a short story about this solitary figure, called a "'peculiar saint'" by Martin Niemöller (De, 291), but the story was never written.

Over a period of at least three years in the late 1950s, Hochhuth continued to research the subject of the "final solution," which had haunted him since the end of the war. As a member of the younger generation he felt an urgent need to ask penetrating questions and find answers. As he himself remembered it in a 1964 interview, the book with the Gerstein report, *Das Dritte Reich und die Juden (The Third Reich and the Jews)* by Leon Poliakov, provided a key, as did another which documented the role of the church during this period.[1]

Daily work on the play began in 1959, including a stay in Rome. In the early stages of its conception, however, the Pope did not figure in the play. But as Hochhuth read more about the Vatican's attitude toward the deportation of Roman Jews in 1943, "it all fitted together like a mosaic." The Pope's dramatic entrance into the play "came about with the consideration — with the question — how, in this so-called Christian Europe, the murder of an entire people could take place without the highest moral authority on this earth having a word to say about it."[2]

25

The choice of the Pope as a central character for the play was a logical one for Hochhuth because of his belief that it is the prominent individuals in history who carry the greatest burden of responsibility (H, 319). Given the author's choice of a traditional dramatic form with a personalization of the conflicts, one might have expected Pope Pius XII to become the protagonist of this "Christian tragedy," as Hochhuth subtitled the play. But the very conclusions that the author drew from his historical research, and elaborated in the "Historical Sidelights" (De, 298–335), made it virtually impossible for him to fill such a role. For what concerned Hochhuth was the Pope's failure to act, his silence. He was, in fact, so convinced by his study of the documentary evidence that the Pope had been passive in this matter that he could not even envisage him as being tragically indecisive — or torn by his choice of alternatives.

As a result, the Pope could not contribute substantially to the dramatic action. But his silence became the subject of much of the dialogue. Nearly all the other characters discuss among themselves, or at least mention, the Pope's failure to speak out directly and forcefully against Hitler's treatment of the Jews, thus leading up to a direct confrontation consisting of a single pivotal scene, the only one in which the Pope himself appears on stage (Act IV).

But the Pope remains a central, albeit stationary, figure, around whom the plot moves topically. Even minor characters sometimes use his inaction as a foil for their actions. Salzer, for example, an SS man who is charged with rounding up the Roman Jews, asks Gerstein: "Am I to be more popish than the Pope?/ If he keeps his mouth shut till evening,/ I've got to load those trains during the night" (De, 188). It is the Pope's inaction that often precipitates the actions of the dual heroes, Kurt Gerstein and Father Riccardo Fontana. In other instances his unseen presence provides the backdrop for individual fates. The Luccani family is arrested literally under the eyes of the Pope, for their apartment looks out on the windows of the Vatican, a fact they explicitly refer to: "The Pope is right beside us;/ with him there,/ no one is going to come and take us away" (De, 128). But they themselves do not believe this, since they are busily packing to go to a monastery when the SS arrive.

The fact that the prominent historical personage who interested Hochhuth could not effectively take the active role he rightly should have had in the plot created a formal dilemma for the author. This was resolved by the creation of a fictional character, the priest Riccardo Fontana, although here too Hochhuth was not without historical models. Both in his "Historical Sidelights" (De, 288–89) and in his dedication, he remembers the Polish Father Maximilian Kolbe, who died as an Auschwitz inmate, and Provost Bernhard Lichtenberg of St. Hedwig's Cathedral in Berlin, who accompanied the Jews at his own request and died on the way to Dachau. Due to his father's position as a lay adviser close to the Pope, Riccardo has direct access to Pius XII, making a personal confrontation dramatically feasible. In this central scene, the Pope momentarily becomes his antagonist, although that dramatic function is shifted to another character, the doctor, in Act V of the play. Riccardo literally becomes the self-appointed "deputy" for the "deputy of Christ" when he tries, by going himself to Auschwitz, to fill the role he feels the Pope has abdicated.

Riccardo's first realization of the facts surrounding the "relocation" of Jews in the East, when Gerstein bursts unannounced into the apartments of the papal nuncio in Berlin (Act I, Scene 1); his subsequent attempts in Rome to get the Pope to speak out (Acts II and III); his eventual failure and his personal decision to wear the Star of David and to join the Roman Jews being deported to Auschwitz (Act IV); his arrival there and his doubting of God's existence in the final confrontation with the devilish, sadistic SS doctor, and with death itself (Act V), constitute the main plot of the play. There are a number of subplots involving Gerstein and the doctor, as well as representatives from all strata of German society, which add depth and breadth to the central one. The drama as a whole provided a wealth of *Zündstoff* (explosive material), but the direct attack on Pius XII, who had died only a few years before, was an unmistakable time bomb.

Those who first read the play realized this fact immediately, and it seemed that the play might never be published or produced. Hochhuth had discussed his work in progress with other authors and with critics, who also recognized the inherent difficulties in trying to bring it to the stage. Its length alone seemed prohibitive, for a full production would last over seven hours. Hans Egon Holthusen helped with suggestions for the versification.[3] Hochhuth had realized that a stylized language — a modified blank verse form — would raise the work above the "Naturalistic" level and would suggest to the reader that the content, although it advanced an historical thesis, was not intended to be a reenactment of history.

But the Rütten and Loening Verlag in Hamburg, which had originally planned to publish it, was forbidden to do so by officials higher up in the Bertelsmann company. The manuscript had already reached the proof stage, but the publisher dutifully destroyed the type.[4] What happened after a copy reached the desk of Heinrich-Maria Ledig-Rowohlt, a more courageous publisher, is told by Erwin Piscator in his introduction to the German edition (St, 7-11; Dr, 7-10). Piscator, like Rowohlt, recognized at once the timeliness of this drama, coming as it did when the Eichmann trial of 1962 was still fresh in people's memory, and the Frankfurt Auschwitz trials were soon to begin.[5] *The Deputy* was just the kind of play Piscator, the new artistic director of the Freie Volksbühne (Free People's Theater), was looking for as the centerpiece of his repertory.

Although not the first to touch this weighty subject matter — Piscator mentions *The Diary of Anne Frank* and *Andorra* in passing — Hochhuth's drama, with its epic dimensions, was reminiscent of Piscator's own attempts in the 1920s to create a documentary, political theater.[6] Piscator's remarks reveal a sense of excitement and a missionary zeal equal to that of his young protégé; "If ever a play appropriately becomes the central point of a repertory that seeks to concern itself with political-historical groups and sequences of events, this is the one! This play makes it worthwhile to produce theater; with this play the theater again gets a mission, a value, becomes necessary."[7]

Piscator was aware, however, that his production of the play at the Theater am Kurfürstendamm in Berlin would be an immediate source for both historical and artistic debate: "I hope that attack and defense of the play will reach *all,* as they have the few who have read it to date; I hope that the value of such a work lies not only in the artistic, the formal, the aesthetic, but first and last in its words and with its reach into life; I hope this play will be a force *for change.*"[8] Yet Piscator considered it his solemn duty to bring this drama to the German stage, no matter what the repercussions. Ledig-Rowohlt knew to whom he was sending the text, for without a man of Piscator's stature, with a strong commitment to a political theater, the play might have been published but never staged. The two men agreed that the date of publication and the premiere should coincide.

## II  *Problems of Form and Content:*
### *Christian Tragedy or Anti-Catholic Polemic?*

Piscator need not have been so concerned that most of the ensuing debate would concentrate solely on aesthetic issues; quite to the contrary, most of the initial reaction focused specifically on Hochhuth's thesis concerning the silence of Pope Pius XII, and primarily attempted to refute the "Historical Sidelights" rather than criticize the play itself.[9] But Piscator's production, which reduced the fifth act to a short epilogue, making Riccardo's development into a tragic hero unclear, contributed directly to this focus. It shifted the emphasis back to the confrontation with the Pope in Act IV and away from the question posed at the beginning of the final act: "Where Are You, God?" (De, 222).[10] To delete the fifth act entirely, however, as many subsequent productions did, is effectively to destroy the plot of the drama and to reduce its claim to being a tragedy. The Pope is not developed at all as a tragic figure, since he is never seen in conflict, and Riccardo only can become one when he puts the existence of God and the meaning of life itself into question at the conclusion of the play. For a tragic fate can only occur when the hero questions the ultimate significance of existence, as Riccardo must when forced by the doctor to work in the crematoriums.[11] But it can be argued that the priest is more a Christian martyr than a tragic hero, since even after this terrible experience his dying words suggest an affirmation of faith: "In hora mortis meae voca me" (De, 283).

Hochhuth eventually submitted to the criticism that Auschwitz could not be portrayed on the stage by writing an alternate conclusion. This variant (Dr, 271–83) was prepared for the production in Basle in September 1963. The author reworked the scene in the Gestapo jail in Rome (Act III, Scene 3) and placed it at the end of the drama instead of Act V. In this version Riccardo is delivered to the SS officer, Salzer, in charge of the roundup of Jews in the Holy City. The latter is visibly nervous about the possibility that some Catholics may have been arrested by mistake, and fearing a protest by the Pope, he gives considerable attention to a young woman, a businessman, and grandfather Luccani, all of whom claim to be Catholics. But strangely, he and his henchmen simply laugh at Father Riccardo. They consider his habit a cheap disguise and hustle him off to exchange his priestly garb for more fitting apparel. The priest is forced to strip the clothes from a corpse lying in the courtyard. But Riccardo disappears from view wordlessly. Hochhuth justified the sudden silence of his otherwise vocal hero as follows: "Riccardo's sense of shame at being a Christian is at this moment as great as his frustration at having failed in his mission" (Dr, 274). The author had apparently abandoned the idea that Riccardo might become a tragic hero: "In the smoke that surrounded the 'final solution' no victim could become a hero. Riccardo disappears forever as a number like everyone else" (Dr, 275). Thus the continued use of the designation "Christian tragedy" in the title would seem to indicate that Hochhuth understood both the Pope's silence and Riccardo's fate as tragic only in the general sense of the word, and not in specifically aesthetic terms.

This alternate conclusion, however, like any deletion of the fifth act, completely undermined the overall structure of the original. For the playwright had carefully arranged his five act drama around the juxtaposition and eventual confrontation of three main groups: the representatives of the church, the Nazis, and the Jews. Act I, subtitled "The Mission," introduces each group by means of a separate scene. The first scene takes place at the papal legation in August 1942. We find Riccardo, newly arrived in Berlin, discussing the wisdom of the Concordat between Hitler and the church with his superior, Cesare Orsenigo. The nuncio points out the need to protect Western civilization from the threat of Russian style communism, even if that means keeping the peace with Hitler. This is an argument that is repeated throughout the play by all representatives of the church, and finally by the Pope himself. This conversation is suddenly interrupted by the entrance of Gerstein, whose urgent message about the gassing of Jews in concentration camps in Poland stuns Riccardo, and lays the groundwork for his "mission." For here Gerstein first introduces the theory that the Pope's intervention would help to improve the situation. Riccardo accepts his evaluation and is determined to return with the message, trusting in the compassion of the Pope and his father's intervention.

Scene two, which has often been compared to the second scene of Carl Zuckmayer's drama *Des Teufels General (The Devil's General),* introduces a cross-section of the Nazi party. The location is a clubroom in a restaurant on the outskirts of Berlin. Hochhuth effectively demonstrates the connection that all the figures have, directly or indirectly, with Auschwitz. In addition to Fritsche and the doctor, members of the SS assigned to Auschwitz, there are the industrialists, like Baron Rutta of the Reichs Armaments Cartel and Müller-Saale of the Krupp works in Essen, who are concerned with the potential labor force that the camp can provide. There is also Professor Hirt, who collects the skulls of victims in order to prove Nazi racial theories; and even the waitress, Helga, has a boyfriend stationed there and decides to accompany the doctor to Auschwitz on his return. Adolf Eichmann is another member of this group, the only strictly historical figure; but all of them, even the sinister doctor, suggest in this harmless setting something of that "banality of evil" of which Hannah Arendt speaks in her book *Eichmann in Jerusalem.* The banality, and horror, of the snippets of conversation, sandwiched between rounds of bowling, eating, and drinking, create a chilling effect. Unfortunately, this scene is often cut by directors who emphasize the conflict between Riccardo and the Pope, thus downplaying the other groups that make up the whole constellation. This scene is particularly crucial because it introduces the camp doctor, whose job it is to sort out the prisoners as they arrive in Auschwitz, determining which ones are fit for work and which ones will go immediately to the gas chambers. Gerstein provides a link with the first scene, and his appearance here completes the sketch of his dual personality. He reports to Eichmann that he was unable to carry out the experiment with a new gas, Cyclon-B, a task he had been assigned as a specialist in disinfection. But this admission immediately arouses suspicion about his loyalty and clearly indicates the perilous route he has chosen in opposing the Nazi rule from within. Another message, delivered by Salzer, is equally important for the development of Hochhuth's thesis. Salzer reports trouble with the church in Slovakia, and the reactions of the Nazis reinforce Hochhuth's theory that they feared the protest of the church.

In the third scene of the first act, the Jews are introduced through the figure of Jacobsen, a young man whom Gerstein has hidden in his Berlin apartment. Both the doctor and Riccardo visit Gerstein, thus providing the configuration of four individuals (doctor, Riccardo, Gerstein, and Jacobsen) who turn up at Auschwitz in the final act. The doctor is already suspicious of Gerstein, so the latter is relieved that the priest does not meet him on the stairs. Riccardo comes to discuss what should be done to help prevent the mass murder and to assure Gerstein that the Pope will speak out.

Gerstein presses him into more immediate service, as the priest reluctantly hands over his passport and habit to Jacobsen, who will try to escape over the Brenner pass under this assumed identity. In return, Riccardo receives the yellow star of David that all Jews were required to wear. Despite Riccardo's general optimism at this point about the role of the church, Gerstein's words presage the final outcome: "I will not survive the work that I must do./ A Christian in these days *cannot*/ survive if he is truly Christian" (De, 79).

The same tripartite structure is repeated in Act III. Here the locale is Rome, as the drama seems to move inward in concentric circles until it reaches the hellish location of ultimate confrontation at Auschwitz. The conflicts between the three groups outlined in Act I are repeated here at a higher level of intensity, and the overlap of representation in each scene is greater, although one group dominates each scene. The order is changed, however. We begin with the Jews. An SS officer, Witzel, and several Italian militia men arrest the Luccani family, thus graphically illustrating the fate of the Jews. The atmosphere here is even more charged than in the Jacobsen scene of Act I, for there escape still seemed possible, whereas here the family is caught before they can flee.

Scene two takes place in a nearby abbey, refuge to a large number of Roman Jews. Riccardo and Gerstein have come to discuss with the abbot and a cardinal what else can be done for them. Both insist that the Pope should protest the action of the Nazis in very clear terms. Riccardo begins to reveal a certain hubris by announcing that, if necessary, he will accompany the victims to their destination, thereby becoming the Pope's "deputy." When Gerstein reveals a daring plan to take over the Vatican radio, Riccardo immediately seconds the idea, demonstrating a fanatical missionary zeal that horrifies both his superiors. The emotionally charged scene ends when Riccardo asks for help but is unable to confess to the abbot, who calls him a murderer and turns away in disgust.

The third scene of this act, set in the *Gestapokeller* in Rome, has already been mentioned. In the original version Riccardo does not appear at all. After the girl, the businessman, and Luccani Sr. have been returned to their cell, Gerstein and the abbot enter to talk to Salzer, whom Gerstein warns about a possible papal protest. But Salzer insists that if such a message is not forthcoming soon he will have to carry out his orders. Gerstein is unable to persuade him that it would be too dangerous in any case, once again pointing to the possible effectiveness of the Pope's protest. The abbot does not give Gerstein's secret away, but, ironically, he has come, not to plead for the Jews, but to ask for the release of a young Italian, a supposed communist, whose father has connections in high places.

Acts II and IV provide a kind of counterpoint, giving the overall structure a balanced — even rhythmic — quality. Each of these acts consists of only one scene in contrast to the tripartite scheme in Acts I, III, and V. Each deals with Riccardo's confrontation with the church authorities. The first, entitled "The Bells of St. Peter's," depicts Riccardo's return to Rome. His father, Count Fontana, counsel to the Holy See, is dismayed when he begs him to use his influence to persuade the Pope to speak out against the Nazi terror. Hochhuth structures the whole confrontation between Riccardo and the church around the principle of gradation. The dispassionate discussion with Orsenigo in Act I, Scene 1, is repeated as an argument with his father here, and in the company of Gerstein at an even more violent level in Act III, Scene 2. A climax is reached in Act IV, when the Pope himself is present. But that scene benefits not so much from any new content as from the dramatic clash of two contrasting personalities: the authoritative, austere, even cold Pius XII and the hot-headed, passionate young priest. The only possible line of defense is already drawn by Fontana in Act II when he explains the Pope's policy of neutrality and his silence as necessary for reasons of state. It is the perennial dilemma of the church, which is both a secular and a religious power. He too raises the specter of Russian victory and domination of Europe, which, to the church, is the greater of two evils. And such an objection seems particularly justified at the moment when the cardinal enters to announce the German defeat at Stalingrad. But his even more exaggerated pro-German stance only enrages Riccardo, forcing the father to take his son's part, as he will in Act IV.

In this pivotal scene, entitled *Il Gran Rifiuto,* words taken from *The Divine Comedy* by Dante, the father and the cardinal first discuss with the Pope what should be done in light of the new arrests of Jews in Rome. Only after they fail to persuade him is Riccardo brought in to tell what he knows; but because of the recent developments, Fontana and the cardinal now seem closer in their sentiments to Riccardo's position. In fact, everyone expects the Pope to do something. Tension is raised to its highest level when the Pope, after explaining his reasons for neutrality, nevertheless begins to dictate a message. But the statement is so general as to apply to all "war crimes". Significantly, it is the cardinal who suggests that the Jews be specifically mentioned, even dictating the words, but the Pope has them stricken. The turning point of the play is thus carefully prepared in terms of both content and form. All the arguments pro and con have been aired long before Riccardo meets Pius XII face to face. And the priest's increasing sense of anger and frustration, which goes hand in hand with the increasing daring of the Nazis, is clearly visible in earlier scenes, making his outburst here believable. Yet despite this preparation and repetition, the moment is nonetheless astonishing and dramatic. It is at this point that Riccardo abandons one mission to take on another, as he raises the yellow star to his breast in front of the Pope and proclaims his intention to follow the Jews: "God shall not destroy His Church/ only because a Pope shrinks from His summons" (De, 220). The Pope's final gesture is equally theatrical; he washes his ink-stained hands, reminding one of Pontius Pilate and suggesting a symbolic denial of responsibility.

From the point of view of both content and form, Act V, then, forms a logical conclusion to the play. Auschwitz is the only place where Riccardo can carry out his new mission. It also brings all three groups represented in the play to a final confrontation; and, divided into three scenes, it rounds out the pattern of point and counterpoint that characterizes the entire dramatic structure. In addition, this final act fashions important links with characters introduced in Acts I and III. Riccardo meets the doctor in the camp for the first time after his arrival in the transport from Rome. With his reappearance and that of Jacobsen, as well as a number of minor characters from the *Jägerkeller* (Act I, Scene 2), a connection is firmly established with the beginning of the play. Similarly, the Luccani family accompanies Riccardo, thus effectively linking Act V to Act III, Scene 1, as well. Gerstein arrives only a short time later, determined to rescue the priest. Fritsche is horrified to learn that a Jesuit has been admitted to the camp and agrees to release him into Gerstein's custody immediately. But then, to Gerstein's surprise, Jacobsen appears when the priest's number is called. As soon as the Jew understands the situation, he begs his former protector to kill him, but when Riccardo arrives on the scene he is determined to save Jacobsen a second time. Before either can escape, however, the doctor intervenes. He arrests Gerstein on the spot. Jacobsen's and Riccardo's attempts to save their friend are futile, and when Riccardo takes aim at the doctor with Gerstein's gun he is killed instantly by machine gun fire. His body is carried off and Gerstein is led away. The play concludes with the ironic commentary that it was Russian soldiers who finally released the surviving inmates in January 1945, without the Pope ever having made a formal protest against the "final solution."

Many critics have insisted on separating the problems of form and content presented by this drama. John Simon, for example, while not entirely discounting the content, concentrates on the formal achievement, praising Hochhuth for reinstating the tragedy as a legitimate form of drama:

> What makes *The Deputy,* as Hochhuth has written it, important, however, is not so much the political revelation it may have made.... What *is* momentous is that in an age which has progressively convinced itself its significant dramatic form is dark comedy, that, to quote Dürrenmatt, "our world has led to the Grotesque as to the atom bomb, just as the apocalyptic pictures of Hieronymus Bosch are grotesque, too" — that in this era when "the death of tragedy" has become a literary commonplace, *The Deputy* stands as a valid tragedy: not great, but good, and anything but commonplace.[12]

Susan Sontag does just the opposite in her thoughtful analysis, concentrating on the impact of the content, while discounting the traditional form in which it was presented: "To read *The Deputy* — I have not yet seen it performed — is an exhausting, an overwhelming, and a tremendously moving experience. But this is, I believe, because of the supreme importance of its content — not because of its style or dramaturgy, both of which are extremely conventional."[13]

But Sontag also agrees with Simon that *The Deputy* is a valid tragedy, albeit in a different sense. "We live in a time in which tragedy is not an art form but a form of history." And the "murder of six million European Jews" is the "supreme tragic event" of our time.[14] Sontag suggests that the Eichmann trial had the function of tragic drama, serving as a means for historical memory, not just for punishment, but to help the audience achieve a catharsis. She argues that the trial, which functioned as a work of art, can be legitimately compared to the drama, *The Deputy:* "Some art — but not all — elects as its central purpose to *tell the truth;* and it must be judged by its fidelity to the truth, and by the relevance of the truth which it tells. By these standards, *The Deputy* is an extremely important play."[15] In the rapidly growing controversy that followed the publication and production of the play, two major groups of critics emerged — those who, like Simon, were primarily concerned with form, and those who, like Sontag, insisted that the importance of the play was its historical fidelity and proceeded to judge it solely on that basis.

At least one critic has suggested that these separate views are more closely linked, however. Manfred Durzak has maintained that by choosing the five act tragedy form with its traditional overtones, Hochhuth was led to the false conclusion that politics in the twentieth century is still primarily a matter of the decisionmaking of individuals, thus overestimating the role of the Pope from the beginning.[16] But Hochhuth's theoretical statements up to this point have demonstrated that the use of such a dramaturgy was not a mere *Hilfkonstruktion* (auxiliary device), as Durzak suggests. The playwright's historical thesis cannot be attributed to a mistaken choice of dramatic form but to a previously held *Weltanschauung* that logically led to that choice. One must therefore proceed to a closer examination of the link between form and content in the drama itself, in order to see whether there are inconsistencies in the use of this dramaturgy that do not conform to Hochhuth's theoretical point of departure, and therefore weaken *The Deputy* not only as a work of art, but as a political statement.

Despite his interest in prominent historical figures like Pius XII, Hochhuth's shift of focus onto an individual fictional hero like Riccardo was not at all inconsistent with his views. As we have seen, he constantly affirmed his belief in the freedom of choice and the concomitant responsibility of all men. Each person, he felt, suffers an individual fate, and thus even the mass murder carried out at Auschwitz had to be portrayed dramatically from the individual's perspective. It is exactly in this spirit that Piscator interpreted the play as one which asks the question of responsibility, not just the Pope's, but that of all human beings.

This play is an historical drama in Schiller's sense. It sees man as acting; and in his actions as a representative, or "deputy," of an *Idea: free* in the fulfillment of this idea, free in his insight into the necessity of *categorically* ethical, essentially human behavior. This freedom which we all possess, which we all possessed under the Nazi regime as well, must be our point of departure if we wish to master our past. To disclaim his freedom would be to disclaim the guilt each took upon himself if he did not make use of his freedom to decide *against* inhumanity.[17]

What both Piscator and Hochhuth seem to ignore, however, is the question of whether the victims of the concentration camps can also be considered to have had a similar opportunity to exercise free choice, whether they can be adequately portrayed in the context of this traditional dramaturgy. While rejecting the concept of mass man, Hochhuth is never able to convince us that what happened at Auschwitz was not mass murder. His inability to translate the victim's experiences into a dramatic form that demands individualization remains one of the major weaknesses of the play. It marks the point at which the content and the form seem to be at odds with each other. Whereas the Pope, Gerstein, Riccardo, and even the SS men are readily shown to be exercising free choice, Hochhuth's attempts to portray the fate of the Jews in the same manner are somewhat unconvincing.

Hochhuth does try to individualize their experience by introducing several subplots. The first is concerned with Jacobsen, who has been hidden in Gerstein's apartment in Berlin (Act I, Scene 3). But after the first act one loses sight of him, until he suddenly reappears in Auschwitz in the last scene, where Hochhuth cleverly uses the problem of double identity as a way of precipitating the final confrontation between Riccardo, Gerstein, and the camp doctor. But his role seems particularly artificial for this very reason, and he is never fully developed as a character.

Hochhuth's second attempt to personalize the fate of the victims is in his presentation of a Jewish family, the Luccanis, who are in the same transport as Riccardo. However, the scenes before their arrest in Rome flounder awkwardly over domestic side issues (De, 130). The only guilt they must assume is that of hesitation in packing to go to a monastery. The author himself seems to have realized that these attempts were inadequate. Thus, at the beginning of Act V, he briefly resorts to a nonindividualized portrayal, by using a short series of monologues on the darkened stage to show the thoughts of the deported Jews in the boxcars on their way to Auschwitz. He specifically requested that there be no attempt to use realistic sound effects, like the crying of children, during this sequence (De, 224). The voices of the anonymous victims speak in lyrical monologues, a significant exception in a drama which is based on the interaction of individuals in dialogue form.

Hochhuth used these monologues not merely to suggest the tragic fate of millions of others, nor simply to create a mood that he hoped to sustain in the following scenes, but also very effectively to link the fourth and fifth acts thematically. One is reminded of the silence of the Pope by an oblique reference to the Vatican Museum and is similarly introduced to the theme of the fifth act, the question of God's silence in the face of this horror: "Cold, God is cold; my hands grow numb/ When I try to fold them to pray with./ And the gods of the ancients are dead as their legends,/ Dead as the antique rubble in the Vatican Museum,/ The morgue of art" (De, 226).[18] This radical departure from the otherwise "realistic" approach to the portrayal of the dramatis personae seems somewhat inconsistent with Hochhuth's belief in the individualization of man's fate; yet, ironically, it is one of the most effective scenes in the play for conveying the fate of the victims.

Hochhuth's use of an allegorical figure offers the most striking example of his departure from "Realism," however. *Der Doktor,* who, unlike the figures in the monologues, plays an important role in the dramatic action, also carries no name. He plays an individualized role, but he is not a person in the same sense as the other characters. Although he too has an historical prototype, Joseph Mengele, the infamous concentration camp doctor, Hochhuth likens him not to Mengele, but to a figure in a medieval morality play:

Because this "doctor" stands in such sharp contrast not only to his fellows of the SS, but to all human beings, and so far as I know, to anything that has been learned about human beings, it seemed permissible to me at least to suggest the possibility that, with this character, an ancient figure in the theater and in Christian mystery plays is once more appearing upon the stage. Since this uncanny visitant from another world was obviously only playing the part of a human being, I have refrained from any further effort to plumb its human features — for these could contribute nothing to our understanding of so incomprehensible a being or its deeds. Seemingly human, the phenomenon of the DOCTOR is in reality comparable to no human being, not even to Heydrich whom Carl J. Burckhardt describes — stylizing him larger than life — as a young, evil god of death. (De, 32–33)

Such an approach seems entirely inconsistent with the author's contention that it is ordinary men placed in positions of responsibility who have chosen for good or evil and are therefore capable of guilt. For this figure is raised above the level of ordinary men, a partial admission by Hochhuth perhaps that his *Weltanschauung* was not entirely adequate to deal with the topic of Auschwitz, neither with the victims, nor with the persecutors. The allegorical function of the doctor, which is emphasized throughout the play, is particularly disturbing in Act V. Here he is the only character who is actually shown to be a persecutor. The other characters are clearly victims, like the Luccanis; people like Gerstein or Riccardo, who seem to have come to Auschwitz by some fatal mistake; Rutta and Müller, who are just passing through on business; or Fritsche, who appears briefly but refuses to come into the inner camp to pick up the priest, thus disassociating himself from the final catastrophe. The commandant does not appear at all, and a minor character like Helga is completely under the spell of the doctor. By removing all the "realistic" characters, especially historical figures like Eichmann, who appears earlier in the play (Act I, Scene 2), from any effective association with the camp, Hochhuth places the entire weight of Auschwitz squarely on the shoulders of a single figure, and, by treating that figure as super — or sub — human, he avoids the question of guilt and responsibility where it seems most crucial.

In yet another instance Hochhuth shows some inconsistency in the application of his premise concerning individual responsibility. Although he had rejected the use of specific devices that would cause *Verfremdung* (alienation) beyond that which was created by the "realistic" treatment of character, time, and place, an acting technique is suggested at the very beginning of the play that would create such an alienation effect. An actor who appears in one scene as a Catholic monk may be an SS man, an Italian soldier, or even a Jew in the next. Even the Pope is grouped in this way; of the male characters, only Riccardo and Gerstein are exempt from this treatment (De, 11). Despite Hochhuth's explanation for the use of this technique, the implication that actors are completely interchangeable is strangely inconsistent with his stated belief that despite the principle of general conscription, which forces men into roles they may not have freely chosen, each individual can still be held responsible for his actions (H, 320).

In still another aspect of the dramatic form, the use of time and place, Hochhuth was not completely able to reconcile form and content. The scenes are ordered according to a linear sequence that is supported by the causal nature of the interaction between characters. Riccardo's meeting with Gerstein in Berlin results in the conversation with his father in Rome in the next act; the Luccani's arrest in Rome is shown, and subsequently their arrival in Auschwitz. This linear approach to time reinforces the "realistic" nature of the drama, and a certain unity is achieved by virtue of the fact that Gerstein and Riccardo appear in all three major locations, Berlin, Rome, and Auschwitz. Hochhuth selected Auschwitz as his setting for the final act because he felt it was the only place where a real confrontation between Riccardo and everything the doctor represented could take place.

What at first appears to have been a good solution, adding to the topical and formal unity of the play, created one of its central dilemmas, however. Hochhuth was faced with the knotty problem of how to present the concentration camp in a realistic fashion on the stage. Up to that point Hochhuth had included extensive descriptions of the stage sets in the text, giving an exact account of costumes and furnishings. But whereas the quarters of the nuntius in Berlin and the hostel in Falkensee, or even the papal apartments, could be easily dealt with in this manner, Auschwitz proved elusive. Hochhuth found it necessary to expound on these difficulties at the beginning of Act V:

The question of whether and how Auschwitz might be visualized in this play occupied me for a long time. Documentary naturalism no longer serves as a stylistic principle. So charged a figure as the anonymous Doctor, the monologues, and a number of other features, should make it evident that no attempt was made to strive for an imitation of reality — nor should the stage set strive for it. On the other hand, it seemed perilous in the drama, to employ an approach such as was so effectively used by Paul Celan in his masterly poem *Todesfuge,* in which the gassing of the Jews is entirely translated into metaphors.

For despite the tremendous force of suggestion emanating from sound and sense, metaphors still screen the infernal cynicism of what really took place — a reality so enormous and grotesque that even today, fifteen years after the events, the impression of unreality it produces conspires with our natural strong tendency to treat the matter as a legend, as an incredible apocalyptic fable. Alienation effects would only add to this danger. No matter how closely we adhere to historical facts, the speech, scene and events on the stage will be altogether surrealistic. (De, 222–23)

Hochhuth was caught in a dilemma. He believed that since Auschwitz had existed one should be able to portray it on stage. But while rightly noting the "Surrealistic" nature of that reality in and of itself, and while pointing out the danger of thinking of Auschwitz as a nightmare, as something unreal or not understandable, he ignored the fact that by introducing the allegorical figure of the doctor he had himself contributed to this tendency. And whereas the monologues at the beginning of Act V did help to make the thematic and scenic transition from Act IV, they did not substantially solve the problem of how to present Auschwitz on stage. As soon as this brief interlude is completed, the lights are raised, and we are returned to a highly "realistic" stage set, which Hochhuth describes painstakingly, while protesting: "What took place in the interior of this underworld, at the crematorium itself, exceeds imagination. There is no way of conveying it" (De, 228).[19]

But Hochhuth still seems to be trying to present the concentration camp in the same way in which he presented scenes in Berlin and Rome. What was acceptable there seems forced here. The author was aware of his ultimate failure, but it is of little help to the potential director when he adds: "It is, however, that constant pall of smoke and fire which makes the stage setting characteristic of Auschwitz. The audience must sense that the dreary hut with its little garden represents a comparatively human façade — but a façade that rather exposes than conceals what goes on behind it" (De, 228). It is significant that Hochhuth makes no practical suggestions as to how the stage set could recreate this atmosphere, other than the use of a cement mixer for monotonous background noise (De, 239). But this device alone cannot hope to evoke the horror of the crematoriums. He ignored the possibility of incorporating actual documentary material by the use of projections or film clips, in the tradition of Piscator's political theater.

It is perhaps because of these difficulties, as well as the overall length of the play, that most productions eliminated all or part of the fifth act, where the problem of uniting form and content became most critical. Thus even in the original five act version, Hochhuth contributed to the transformation of his play by many directors from a Christian tragedy, as first conceived, into an anti-

Catholic polemic. This was particularly true of the sensationalized adaptation of Jerome Rothenberg used in the New York production by Herman Shumlin (Brookes Atkinson Theater, February 1964).[20]

But even in book form, some critics argued, Hochhuth's play was basically a polemic. A typical commentary of this kind by Rolf C. Zimmermann argued that the drama was not a tragedy at all, but a series of scenes "consisting of experimental moral tests,"[21] and that Riccardo was merely a "figure of demonstration," not a tragic hero.[22] Zimmermann emphasized the influence of Brecht, incorrectly I think, but he pointed out in his conclusion an important aspect of any evaluation of *The Deputy*. Being basically "polemical," this drama has a significance quite apart from any poetic considerations:

We ordinarily distrust widespread influence when it is a question of poetic claims. But we can hardly ignore the fact that the widespread effect of *The Deputy* is not poetic and not even that of a "hit." Neither the one nor the other expands its audience through discussion, but steals its way into favor on soft shoes quite unlike the polemic. Quarrels about taste are short-lived, those about a "cause," on the other hand, go on forever. And while with poetry the extent of its effect is irrelevant, with the polemic — precisely for the sake of its cause — it is a sign of its quality.[23]

Thus even in those circles where the chief concern was aesthetic, the conclusion was often drawn, as Piscator had hoped it would be, that *The Deputy,* whether tragedy or polemic, was an *important* play — if not a great one — because of its impact and the debate which it engendered.

### III   *The Widening Circles of Dispute*

Now, over ten years later, it is somewhat difficult to imagine the furor that surrounded the premieres of *The Deputy* in Berlin and other cities around the world. The play was translated almost immediately into a dozen languages, and other directors of stature — Ingmar Bergmann (Dramaten, Stockholm, 1963); Peter Brook (Théâtre Athénée, Paris, 1964); Clifford Williams (Royal Shakespeare Company, London, 1965) — took on the challenge of making this mammoth work stageable. Of the West German productions (Frankfurt, Essen, Düsseldorf, Hamburg, Bochum) significantly, none took place in the southern, Catholic regions. Hochhuth at first refused to have the work published or performed in the East, for fear it would be misinterpreted and used as propaganda against the West, but by 1966 he had reversed his position, and the play was also produced in Dresden, Rostock, and Leipzig, and at the Deutsches Theater in East Berlin, under the direction of Hans-Dieter Meves and Friedo Solter.[24]

Public protests accompanied the abortive attempt to produce the play successfully in Basle, Switzerland. When the Swiss government refused to ban the play outright, the opposition turned to massive demonstrations. Two hundred policemen were needed to provide security on opening night. Each of the seventeen performances was interrupted, whereupon the play was removed from the repertory.[25] Similar street demonstrations accompanied the opening on Broadway in March 1964, just a little over a year after the Berlin premiere. On that occasion, the audience was not allowed to leave the building during the intermission, as members of the American Legion and the American Nazi Party marched side by side, calling the author the "Antichrist," while mounted police tried to keep order.[26]

But such visible signs of controversy represented only the tip of the iceberg. The real "storm" over Hochhuth's drama raged not in the streets, but in the press. Many different voices were raised, Catholic, Jewish, Protestant and nondenominational. But the pros and cons did not divide themselves strictly according to religious views. Some writers defamed the author, accusing him of "character assassination,"[27] others simply lauded Pius XII, while still others felt it necessary to rush to Hochhuth's — rather than the Pope's — defense.[28]

The Catholic church was not slow to react. Only a few days after the premiere in Berlin, a response by Pius XII's personal secretary, Father Robert Leiber, a German Jesuit, was published in the *Frankfurter Allgemeine Zeitung*. Leiber pointed out the Pope's charitable acts toward the Jews during the war period and countered Hochhuth's challenge with the thesis that had the Pope spoken out more directly he would have brought on even worse reprisals.[29] More significantly, Cardinal Montini, soon to become Pope Paul VI, submitted an open letter to the British journal, *The Tablet,* in June of that year, offering a similar argument. Hochhuth replied directly, outlining the main points of disagreement between himself and the church. Admittedly, Montini had only secondhand knowledge of the play, relying on reviews in the press for his impression of it. "The image of Pius XII which Hochhuth presents, or is said to present, is a false one," he wrote. The Pope, according to Montini, had been neither cowardly nor heartless, nor had his attitude been "inspired by a calculating political opportunism."[30] Montini, like Leiber, argued that Hochhuth had overlooked completely that "an attitude of protest and condemnation such as this young man blames the Pope for not having adopted would have been not only futile but harmful."[31] But the cardinal, without proving his point, proceeded to make the erroneous assumption, as did many of Hochhuth's critics who had not actually read the play, that the author was, by focusing on the guilt of the Pope, trying to divert guilt away from the Germans themselves.

Hochhuth's reply offered no new insights, however. He quoted from his "Historical Sidelights" concerning the role that Montini had played in those days as undersecretary of state. And he continued to disagree on the point that a protest could only have brought worse reprisals. What imaginable fate could have been worse than the one the Jews had already been subjected to? After citing an instance in which two Jews had been released by the Gestapo, simply because the Pope had "unofficially" requested it, he asked rhetorically: "Would an *official* protest in the presence of the entire world, or even the threat of one, have been completely ineffective?"[32] Hochhuth had no doubts as to the answer, and it remained the central — ultimately unanswerable — question around which a great deal of the debate revolved. Hochhuth himself was partially responsible for confusing historical analysis of what did happen with speculative debate about what might have happened.

By no means all Catholics considered the play to be dangerous to the church. One Catholic historian, for example, called it a "creative provocation," which ought to lead Catholics to "the necessary discussion of the firmly-entrenched tradition of the Church: Should the Church continue to regard itself, as it has since the Counter-Reformation, as a fortress which, in defending its own 'holy interests,' ignores the life, suffering and death of people of different views? Or should the Church — Mother Church — be conceived of as the matrix of mankind, open, protective of all the children of men?"[33] But the blind outrage expressed in Cardinal Spellman's press release at the time of the New York premiere is certainly more typical.[34]

The involvement of historians, philosophers, journalists, literary and drama critics, as well as the church hierarchy, in the debate was so intense and so extensive that only a brief summary can be given here of its scope and content. When the Rowohlt Verlag decided to publish an overview of the most important contributions in June 1963, only four months after the Berlin premiere, there were over three thousand comments to choose from.[35] A similar flood of literature surrounding the New York production is recorded in the bibliography, compiled by David Beams, at the conclusion of *The Storm over the Deputy*.[36] Distinguished voices were raised in Hochhuth's defense, those of Albert Schweitzer, whose letter to Rowohlt provided the introduction to the American edition and Karl Jaspers among them.[37]

Two positive critiques, by Golo Mann and Walter Muschg, were included in the 1972 edition of Hochhuth's *Dramen* and are representative of favorable reviews. Mann, a noted German historian, went beyond the historical dispute over whether a formal protest by the Pope could have improved — or worsened — the situation, to suggest that Hochhuth's "real accomplishment" had been to deal with history in an artistic form. "How much perception of things human, how much empathy, fantasy and pity, sorrow, deep revulsion and anger are forced under the yoke of art."[38] Quoting from the Eichmann verdict, Mann suggested that the depiction of the human dimensions of the horror was a task appropriate only to "'great writers.'"[39] While reserving final judgment on whether Hochhuth qualified as a "great" writer, Mann praised his struggle with this particular subject matter, noting its effect on the German public — which had been more far-reaching than any of the exhaustive historical studies — as evidence of its high achievement.[40]

Walter Muschg echoed Golo Mann when he maintained that the ultimate worth of this drama must be ascertained by evaluating its effect, reminding the reader that Dürrenmatt's *Die Physiker* (*The Physicists*) and Ionesco's *Nashörner* (*Rhinoceros*) had not aroused nearly the same response.[41] Unlike most literary critics however, Muschg defended Hochhuth's dramaturgy, maintaining that negative evaluations of it "reveal how deeply buried is the tradition of a free, polemical literature in Germany, which leads from the Enlightenment via Young Germany to Expressionism" (Dr, 285).[42] Muschg compared the furor over Lessing's *Nathan der Weise* (*Nathan the Wise*), which was not performed in the author's lifetime, with the furor over the *The Deputy,* drawing a specific parallel between the audience scenes in both plays: "It is ridiculous to call here for better psychology or more historical accuracy. Such art is concerned with a kind of truth which no psychologist and no historian can reveal" (Dr, 286). Muschg even went so far as to defend the much maligned fifth act. With his search for an absolute moral confrontation, he argued, Hochhuth had no choice but to present Auschwitz on stage and to use an allegorical devil figure like the doctor. Muschg praised Hochhuth as a dramatist who, with his return to a traditional dramaturgy, had rejected the "antidrama" of the "Theater of the Absurd" or the "Grotesque," and had provided a conservative, yet revolutionary alternative (Dr, 287).

Another different, yet representative, response to the play is that of Wilhelm Alff, in an article entitled "Richtige Einzelheiten — Verfehltes Gesamtbild" ("Correct Details — Incorrect General Picture"), which first appeared in the *Frankfurter Allgemeine Zeitung* on May 11, 1963. Hochhuth replied on May 30 with an article, "Ein Gesamtbild gibt es nicht" ("There is no general picture"), to which Alff responded several days later.[43] Alff's title reveals a typical approach; he did not question the accuracy of the documentary evidence Hochhuth had used in his "Historical Sidelights," but, after suggesting that a false conclusion had been drawn, he used the same evidence to draw a different one. Alff argued that it was necessary for the Pope, above all, to preserve the neutrality of the church. Thus he could say of Hochhuth: "On the basis of largely correct sources, Hochhuth draws a false picture. The unclear sources on which he draws are not those of the documents, but those of his own false consciousness."[44]

Hochhuth's response was equally vehement, protesting that Alff, like so many of his critics, had misunderstood the thesis of the play to begin with. The thesis was not that if Pius XII had spoken out, extermination of the Jews would necessarily have been stopped outright by the Nazis, but rather that the Pope, as leader of the Catholic church, should at least have made an attempt to persuade Hitler — that it was his moral obligation as "Vicar of Christ" to do so (K, 182). This position is clearly reflected in the choice of a quote from Albert Camus as a motto for the American edition of the play: "Who are we, anyway, that we dare criticize the highest spiritual authority of the century? Nothing in fact, but the simple defenders of the spirit, who yet have a right to expect the most from those whose mission it is to represent the spirit'' (De, 3).

The author continued to insist that additional documentary evidence he had received since the premiere had merely substantiated his original thesis. Even more importantly for an understanding of Hochhuth's continuing artistic efforts, the young moralist defended his position that prominent personages do make history. For Hochhuth this too was seen as a moral issue. ''That touches on a very interesting moral problem: whether or not, as a fashionable opinion and therefore Alff would have it, that it is of no historical consequence, *who* governs; whether or not historical events occur independently of the *person* who sets them in motion; whether or not one can even consider them, without taking into consideration the character of their protagonists'' (K, 189). Throughout the period of controversy, Hochhuth simply reaffirmed his historical thesis and his basic position that one must view history in terms of individual protagonists — a Pope Pius XII, a Churchill, even a Hitler — thus reaffirming at the same time his choice of a traditional dramaturgy. He also reiterated his belief that, despite the importance of historical accuracy and documentation, the drama has a moral truth of its own, not to be confused with historical truth. Hochhuth did not change his point of view at all during the years following the publication of his first drama, but defended it tirelessly against all opponents, while working on a second one.

## CHAPTER 3

# Soldiers: Obituary for Geneva

## I  *Another "Gathering Storm"*

T HE "storm" over *The Deputy* had hardly abated when the clouds of another controversy began to gather. Yet it was 1967 before the storm was unleashed by Hochhuth's second drama, *Soldaten: Nekrolog auf Genf*. The seed for this play had already been sown during the period when the author was researching *The Deputy*, but the virulent attack on that play by some critics made him hesitate to embark on another such historical quest. He even talked of writing a comedy.[1] Adverse publicity also contributed to his decision to move to a suburb of Basle, Switzerland, with his wife, Marianne, and their two sons.

At first Hochhuth wished to explore the problem of the soldier in modern warfare, consciously borrowing the title from his *Sturm und Drang* counterpart, Reinhold Michael Lenz.[2] He had already touched on the problem of the soldier in a period of general conscription in *The Deputy,* implying the ultimate responsibility of every soldier for his acts, but in *Soldiers* he intended to focus specifically on aerial warfare. In Hochhuth's view, the practice of bombing civilian centers during World War II, a tactic used by both the Germans and the Allies, made the soldier-pilot a potential war criminal. The bomber pilot who had dropped the atom bomb over Hiroshima was as responsible in his way as President Truman was for issuing the order (K, 117). This opinion is briefly noted in the "Historical Sidelights": "Both sides committed nefarious crimes in the air war against open cities" (De, 330).

Although both Churchill and the Polish general Sikorski, the two key figures in *Soldiers,* are mentioned in *The Deputy* (De, 106,

317), it is a statement by Riccardo's father which most clearly reveals the theme of the next play in incipient form. In discussion with the Pope in Act IV he argues: "Your Holiness, I too was sadly disappointed that it [the Pope's Christmas message] remained without effect. However, in that message Your Holiness did not, unfortunately, mention the Jews *expressis verbis* — nor, I might add, the terror bombing of open cities. It seems to me that anything addressed to Hitler and to Churchill requires words so blunt as not to be misunderstood" (De, 201).

Despite the apparent link suggested here between Hitler and Churchill, Hochhuth did not consider them as equals. For him Hitler was a sick, fanatic criminal who could never serve as a tragic hero, whereas Churchill was the savior of Europe to whom Germans owed a debt of gratitude, but who had nevertheless made tragic mistakes.[3] Although Hochhuth's point of departure had been the individual soldier, the dramatist once again gravitated toward the great personalities of recent history to give substance to his portrayal of the conflict of ideas. But if the material itself and Hochhuth's view of history and drama immediately suggested Churchill as a possible protagonist, it was the reading of David Irving's *The Destruction of Dresden* that provided the missing antagonist. Here Hochhuth first encountered the figure of Bishop Bell of Chichester, who had been vehemently opposed to the bombing of German cities by the RAF.[4] Bell bore a striking resemblance to Father Riccardo, and Hochhuth thought that a confrontation over the issue of air warfare between Churchill and Bell might provide a dramatic climax similar to that which had been achieved by the bringing together of the fictional Riccardo and the Pope.

More important than this discovery, however, was Hochhuth's strong personal opposition to air warfare as it had been practiced during World War II, an opposition that he had first articulated as a youth. He realized that it was not simply an historic issue, but still the basis of military practice, and he hoped his play would help to change that. He first aired his opinions in a letter to Heinrich Lübke in 1964, pleading with the then President of the Federal Republic of Germany to throw his personal weight behind a proposal for an international law — as an addition to the Geneva and Hague agreements on land and sea warfare — that would provide protection for both pilots and civilians (K, 106–29).

This letter reveals the source of the subtitle given the play then in progress, for the "obituary for Geneva" refers to the tragic inability of the International Red Cross to achieve such a convention. The proposal to limit air warfare passed at the 1957 conference in New Delhi had never been ratified, and the bombing of cities continued to be an accepted military strategy, as the Vietnam War was proving. Hochhuth implied the relevance of his position with regard to the war in Southeast Asia only indirectly. Instead he concentrated on past and future examples that would be more likely to move the President. He cited the bombing of Dresden and Hamburg and envisioned the possibility — should there ever be another military confrontation in Europe — that a West German bomber pilot might be expected to drop bombs on East German civilians (K, 126).

Although Hochhuth acknowledged that the Nazis had initiated this strategy with their demolition raid of Rotterdam, he also argued that such civilian bombing had not been considered a war crime at Nuremberg, because it was principally the Allies who had used it during the war. As a result, the aerial bombardment of cities had become the major postwar strategy of both East and West in the atomic "cold war," since theoretically such bombs would also be directed at large population centers (K, 112). Hochhuth did not suggest that it would be possible to end war entirely, but he argued that it was possible to humanize it by returning to a clear differentiation between combatants and noncombatants. In so doing, he overlooked the difficulty of making such distinctions in guerilla warfare.

In his letter to Lübke, Hochhuth revealed his ambivalent attitude toward Churchill. "We Germans, first and foremost, will always be indebted to this figure of the century, because he — next to the Russian soldiers — must take the most credit for the liberation of Europe from this Hitler, for whom we are responsible. But may the evil spirit of Dresden, the horrible mistakes of Churchill, which brought death to innumerable civilians, without contributing to the Allied victory, be buried with him" (K, 129).[5] It also reflected Hochhuth's continuing tendency to consider prominent political leaders as the makers of history, not simply because of the importance he assigned to Churchill, but because of his rather naive belief that Lübke could personally bring about a change in international law.[6] Hochhuth did not modify his views, and he sent the letter a second time to the President — then Gustav Heinemann—

in 1971, when it was published in his collection of essays, *Krieg und Klassenkrieg (War and Class War).*[7]

The importance that Hochhuth attributed to this cause is demonstrated by his assertion that his second drama was "a continuation by other means — theatrical means — of the struggle of the Red Cross to create international conventions governing air warfare."[8] In trying to present his plea using theatrical means, however, Hochhuth was faced with other problems. "I soon realized that it is very difficult for a playwright to dramatize the war in the air; it's too abstract, like submarine warfare. On the stage only human beings are effective; a problem that can't be personalized remains an intellectual puzzle."[9] Not only the need to personalize the problem, but also Hochhuth's growing fascination with the man, contributed to his choice of the prime minister as the central figure of the play. But more historical research was needed before the idea that had been germinating since the 1960s could bear fruit.

The playwright proceeded during 1964 and 1965 to read an enormous amount of material about Churchill and the air war. Then, seemingly by chance, he met a former member of the British Secret Service who told him that the mysterious death of General Sikorski in a plane crash off Gibraltar on July 4, 1943, had been an act of British sabotage. With the discovery of the mass graves of Polish officers at Katyn earlier that year, Sikorski — suspecting the Russians — had demanded an investigation by the Red Cross, thereby straining the alliance between Churchill and Stalin. Hochhuth had his secret source testify under oath and deposited copies of the affidavit in several Western European banks. The contents were to be published only after fifty years.[10] He also enlisted the help of historian David Irving in collecting further circumstantial evidence. Irving's book about Sikorski's death, ironically entitled *Accident,* was published the same day as the Berlin premiere of *Soldiers* — October 9, 1967.[11]

The Sikorski affidavit provided a different theme altogether for the play — the supposed complicity of Churchill in this act of sabotage — but although discussion of the Sikorski subplot predominated in the pre- and postpremiere publicity, it remains secondary to that of civilian bombing in the play itself. The manuscript was completed by Christmas 1966. Hochhuth had hoped for a world premiere in the British National Theatre, but censorship there, and the sudden death of Erwin Piscator, who had planned to produce the play in Berlin, delayed its staging. It seems fitting that the play was first performed in the Freie Volksbühne, albeit under the direction of Hans Schweikart, and that Hochhuth dedicated the play to his mentor, Piscator. In the few years since the aging director had dared to bring *The Deputy* to the stage he had also been responsible for the premieres of several other "documentary" pieces, such as Heinar Kipphardt's *In der Sache J. R. Oppenheimer (In the Case of J. R. Oppenheimer)*, 1964; and Peter Weiss' Auschwitz play, *Die Ermittlung (The Investigation)*, 1965.

In his obituary for Piscator, however, Hochhuth tried to distinguish Piscator's efforts from the often loosely applied formula "documentary theater": "Piscator never meant that documentation was already art, that unfiltered historical rubble, if one merely shoveled it onto the stage, would already create a scene, or that the slogans of the activists would already be language. The *study* of reality, not its 'incorporation' [*Einblendung*], as one presently says, not its reenactment was for Piscator one prerequisite — just one! — of his political art" (H, 458).[12] What Hochhuth attributes here to Piscator, applied in fact to his own attitude toward the use of history in drama. While insisting again and again on the importance of studying history, as an author he felt free to invent scenes and characters, so long as he remained faithful to the events.[13] There is no such thing as pure documentation for Hochhuth. "I am not interested in documents so much; the documents are merely the raw material, the bricks with which one builds a play. One collects the bricks, but merely as means to an end, in order to erect a structure."[14]

## II  *Churchill and Everyman: "Documentary Drama" and Medieval Mystery Play*

Having carefully collected the "bricks," Hochhuth was ready to erect a structure, but he had two different "buildings" in mind (Churchill/Bell and Churchill/Sikorski), as well as two "architectural styles." The resulting ambiguities in content and form reveal a gradual change in the young playwright's concept of political theater. Hochhuth had intended *Soldiers,* like *The Deputy,* to be a tragedy.[15] In addition to the subtitle, "Obituary for Geneva," he used the designation "Tragödie" on the title page. But the term "tragedy" is only applicable, as in the case of *The Deputy,* in the very general sense that it is a dramatic representation of a serious action which turns out disastrously for at least one of the main characters. The use of this designation may also indicate — although Hochhuth nowhere states this specifically — that the action should arouse in the audience a reaction more akin to Aristotelian "catharsis" and "identification" than to the more distancing reaction called for by Brecht's "epic theater." It also suggests a more conventional use of plot and characterization, similar to that found in *The Deputy.* In fact, in his second play Hochhuth faced some of the same problems as in the first, especially after he realized from his extensive reading on the subject that the decisions made by Churchill had been complex: "I soon saw that one can only be fair to Churchill, and to the British and Americans in general, by regarding the bombing war not in isolation but as a part of the total nature of the war. And that led to my writing yet another play of marathon length."[16]

The need to include so much historical background once again added to the length of the play.[17] But Hochhuth had more difficulty this time in integrating the various thematic strands while preserving his original intent to agitate in favor of an air war convention. Although he felt that Churchill had made tragic mistakes, he admired the man greatly and considered the bombing war to have been excusable, even necessary at first: "The bombing was all that Churchill had to offer Stalin in the way of a second front, before Montgomery destroyed Rommel's army in the desert." But such a strategy, he maintained, was inexcusable in our day: "I believe that the man who first tried it out, namely Churchill, was more justified in making mistakes than the strategists of today. Once it has been demonstrated that the sacrifice of 700,000 civilians, 56,000 British pilots, not to mention 44,000 American pilots, was in no way decisive in the Second World War, no air strategist can any longer believe that the bombardment, say, of Vietnamese villages today can bring about a decision on the battlefield."[18]

Thus it was only the discovery of the Sikorski material that enabled Hochhuth to write something akin to tragedy, for this "murder," more than the bombing, suggested a tragic dilemma on Churchill's part.[19] Of the two men — Churchill and Sikorski — only the latter could be a tragic hero, however, for as the prime minister says in the play, "the man who survives a tragedy is not its hero" (S, 152). Yet Hochhuth did not want to abandon his original

intention in favor of a "cloak and dagger" plot. The addition of
the Sikorski subplot, however, suggested the need for a more complex dramatic structure. Thus, the composition of *Soldiers* differs
from the rather conventional five act tragedy format which Hochhuth had used in *The Deputy*. It consists of a framework called
*Everyman* and a three act play-within-the-play entitled *The Little
London Theater of the World*.[20] Since these are two distinct enti-
ties, many directors radically cut or eliminated the framework,
leading to an interpretation of *Soldiers* as a strictly historical or
"documentary drama" and ignoring its just claim to being a symbolic mystery play as well. Once again, the excessive length of the
play and the subsequent need for editing contributed directly to the
emphasis on the historical accuracy of the drama by the critics. In
this case, necessary cuts often detracted from the main issue by
dissolving the link with the present that the frame had established.

The play-within-the-play epitomizes the historical period from
April to July 1943. In Act I, Churchill is seen aboard a British
battleship on the way to Scapa Flow in the North Sea, accompanied
by political associates and aids. A rather extraordinary device is
suggested by Hochhuth at the begining of his stage directions which
was intended to depersonalize the characters: "A cyclorama is
recommended, lit from upstage, so that when we first see the actors
they are depersonalized, little silhouettes in front of the stabbing
duck-egg colored light as it floods into the auditorium — like
marionettes in the hands of an unseen director. This ties in with this
old-fashioned attempt to make the boards of a stage the platform
for the *theatrum mundi*. Only later is the light reduced sufficiently
for us to be able clearly to perceive the individuality of these
figures, their characters and gestures" (S, 65). This indicates a brief
attempt on the part of the author to move away from a strictly
Naturalistic approach to characterization to a symbolic one. But
the lengthy descriptions of the individual characters that immediately follow, as well as their treatment in the dialogue, soon shifts
the reader's or viewer's attention back to Hochhuth's usual perspective. These are not puppets, but individuals in positions of
power, free to choose.

Both the Churchill/Bell and the Churchill/Sikorski material is
introduced in this opening act. First the arguments concerning the
air war, pro and con, are raised as Churchill listens attentively to
his minister of defense, Lord Cherwell, who outlines a plan for the

saturation bombing of German cities. Hoping to bill this as the opening of a second front, the prime minister approves the plan for firestorms to be created in densely populated areas, despite the hesitation of the chief of the general staff, Brooke, who, as a military man, objects to the use of civilian targets and questions the strategic value of the operation. But Churchill goes ahead, assigning the code name Gomorrah to the proposed firebombing of Hamburg. The subplot is introduced when General Sikorski himself appears in the company of Kocjan, a captain in the Warsaw Underground Army. The latter has already initiated a shipboard romance with the prime minister's personal secretary, Helen, a widow, and second officer in the Women's Royal Naval Service. This sub-subplot provides a third strand which runs throughout the play-within-the-play.

As head of the Polish government in exile, Sikorski immediately raises the issue of his country's border dispute with the Soviet Union. Churchill had already tacitly agreed to surrender the eastern Polish lands to Russia, in hopes that the Poles would be able to get an equivalent territorial settlement with Germany in the west after the war. Now the discovery of the mass graves at Katyn has added fuel to the fire. Sikorski tells Churchill that he has already demanded an investigation by the Red Cross, a move which further jeopardizes the alliance between Great Britain and the USSR. Churchill argues eloquently for compromise: "If you do not acquiesce, then Poland will/ be no more — no more than a bloody mire on the tracks of the tanks of the armies of Russia" (S, 119). But Sikorski is adamant, refusing to make any compromises. What Churchill views as "reasonable" demands (S, 112), Sikorski sees as leading to the dismemberment of his country: "That I have been defeated — may be true, but, since it is not *right,* I shall fight on" (S, 117). This demonstration of quixotic determination provides the background for understanding the need to do away with Sikorski, who can only be a thorn in Churchill's side, threatening to tear apart the alliance.

Act II shows the prime minister in bed, nevertheless discharging the duties of his office. Again, the two main themes of the previous act are repeated — the air war and the difficulties with Poland. First, the photos of operation Gomorrah are brought in, and Churchill looks at them eagerly and approvingly. Here the way is briefly prepared for the entrance of Bishop Bell in Act III; for Churchill, knowing of his opposition to the bombings, tells Helen to invite him to come to his country estate sometime (S, 149). The bishop's protest over Gomorrah, as well as that of a member of parliament, provides an opportunity for the prime minister to speak of the Pope, thus serving as a flashback to *The Deputy:*

> Stokes [the MP] I shall not receive — as a Catholic
> he is simply playing the organ for Rome.
> I shall speak to him, when and not before
> Pius protests against the extermination of the Jews.
> We have told the Cardinal Secretary of State,
> several times already, through Osborn,
> that the Eternal Speechifier should actually *say* something
> but he only makes himself clear,
> when he is objecting to air raids. (S, 149)

Word is also brought during this act that Stalin has broken off diplomatic relations with Poland, further exacerbating the situation. The text of the Russian cable suggests that "steps" should be taken "toward the improvement of the constitution of the present Polish government" (S, 159). Lord Cherwell, who is present, notes that "a patriot who has lost his country must lose his life" (S, 159). And it is the diabolical defense minister — reminiscent, in his black cloak, of the doctor in *The Deputy* — who suggests a plan for doing away with Sikorski. By his silence and his gestures Churchill seems to agree to the plan to eliminate the Polish general by means of a crash off Gibraltar.

In the final act of the play-within-the-play, both plots unite in a joint climax in the form of a double confrontation with Churchill. Again, as in *The Deputy,* Hochhuth works with the principle of repetition. The arguments first raised by Brooke in Act I against the saturation bombing of cities are now reiterated by Bishop Bell at a higher level of intensity achieved through his sense of moral outrage as a religious leader. He meets Churchill in the garden at Chequers, as the prime minister had requested. But Churchill tries to avoid him. An RAF pilot, Dorland, the main character in the framework of *Soldiers,* takes part in the conversation, as does Helen, whose husband was a pilot. Significantly, Bell addresses the central question of the play to the newly decorated Dorland, not to the prime minister: "May I ask you: Is a pilot who bombs/ population centers under orders/ still to be called a *soldier*?" (S, 192). All during this lengthy conversation, Churchill has his mind on other matters. He even walks away, leaving Dorland and Helen to carry on for him. Messages unrelated to the plot are delivered, including the word that the German battleship *Scharnhorst* has surrendered (S, 229). But Bell continues his own relentless attack, which parallels the reports about the sea battle:

> Sir, what is an anti-social man compared with an officer
> who persuades himself and his men, by whatever argument,
> to aim at cities — to annihilate them?
> The chances of survival for mankind
> lie in the personal choice of every man,
> each single individual — who on his own instinct,
> or as a mercenary — purposely takes the lives
> of noncombatants.
> The reason does not bear discussion —
> a reason can always be found. (S, 235)

But despite his eloquence the bishop never manages to get the prime minister's undivided attention, and the voice of "reason" — *Staatsräson* — seems to have the upper hand over the uncompromising man of God when the prime minister finally shows him out (S, 237).

The conversation between Bell and Churchill, which takes up nearly the entire act, is punctuated with numerous interruptions, the most dramatic being the announcement of Sikorski's death. Kocjan, who is on hand to say goodby to Churchill *and* Helen before setting out on a dangerous mission to recover a German rocket from behind the lines, uses this opportunity to confront the prime minister directly, thus bringing the subplot to a climax. Again, the author uses the technique of repetition, only here the order of the degrees of intensity is reversed. Kocjan first explodes in front of Helen, convinced that the general has been murdered by the British:

> Yes — Sikorski!
> You murdered him — we Poles,
> everywhere we are in enemy territory.
> No one wants us, everyone uses us —
> like the Jews, a people without a country,
> abandoned, crushed — and yet

> the avalanche shall crush the Germans
> who have set it rolling. (S, 241)

The captain is more subdued in his subsequent confrontation with Churchill, but his is an eloquent, accusing silence. The prime minister flounders for words and "wishes the Pole would turn and go" (S, 248). In this instance it is Kocjan who is the apparent victor, although the accusation against Churchill is left in abeyance.

Hochhuth faced some of the same problems in the play-within-the-play in *Soldiers* as he had had in writing *The Deputy,* due to his presentation of a well-known and well-loved historical personage. This time, however, the author himself was much more sympathetic toward his character, and although he claimed that he wanted to avoid "petty naturalism" (*Anekdoten-Naturalismus*) (S, 165; So, 126), his fascination for "Old Winnie" led him to include a great deal of anecdotal information, lending to the figure of Churchill an aspect of authenticity which reinforced the tendency to treat the play as "documentary drama." This trend toward naturalism, which suggested reenactment, was heightened in both the London and New York productions by the actor, John Colicos, who looked like, and impersonated, the prime minister.[21]

Still another problem in using Churchill as the central figure of a play about the bombing war resembled that which Hochhuth had confronted with Pope Pius XII in *The Deputy.* His historical research had convinced him that the prime minister had not hesitated to order the bombing of Hamburg or Dresden. Thus, the dramatic action could not consist of his inner conflict over the decision. At first Hochhuth thought that the meeting with Bishop Bell would solve this problem, embodying in dramatic terms a conflict of ideas that had existed between them, although such a discussion had never taken place. It was to be the turning point of the dramatic action, but Bell was never fully integrated into the play. Like the Pope, he appears only once — in the third act of the play-within-the-play — but Bell does not even become the major subject of discussion, as the Pope had been. The rather belated appearance of the original antagonist was due to the fact that Hochhuth, and the dramatic action, had gotten irretrievably sidetracked onto the Sikorski subplot.

Critical confusion over Hochhuth's attitude toward history and the documentary nature of his drama was enhanced not only by his treatment of the dramatis personae, but also by his realistic use of time and place. *Soldiers* has often been analyzed as a kind of historical reenactment, despite the author's insistence — even in the text of the play — that it was not:

But this is not science, this is theater, and the only thing that gives one courage is that between the reality of which the stage by its very nature can only reproduce a modest reflection, between history and ourselves, we can place the actor. The bedroom, therefore, like the ship in Act One, should emphasize rather than conceal the fact that we are in a theater. (S, 127)

Despite this avowed rejection of Naturalism, as in *The Deputy,* Hochhuth went to great lengths to describe the settings for all three acts in minute detail: the deck of the HMS "Duke of York" (Act I; S, 65); the bedroom referred to above (Act II; S, 123); and the garden of Chequers (Act III; S, 173), although he noted that the latter scene should be "an ironic reproach" (S, 173) in order to suggest how far man has come from the Garden of Eden. But without the benefit of Hochhuth's commentary the audience can easily accept them as realistic *Schauplätze* (scenes), especially if the set designer does so.

Time is also treated realistically and linearly in the three act Churchill drama, revealing little change from *The Deputy.* The first act gives an exposition of the problems. By the second act some time has elapsed; operation Gomorrah has been carried out, and the plot to kill Sikorski is set in motion. Then, in the third act, the cause-effect pattern is repeated as both plots culminate — the main plot with Bishop Bell's weakly motivated appearance, and the subplot more convincingly with the announcement of Sikorski's death. Significantly, no final answer to the questions raised by the Churchill/Bell debate is given to the audience. Instead the spectator is provoked to think about the opposing arguments. Hochhuth's theater remains nonpartisan here, although he himself had a very definite position on the issue, which he had made clear in his letter to President Lübke. He presents the conflict of ideas in the play-within-the-play, but does not take sides.

The framework of the play offers a very different perspective, however, and introduces an apparently new element into Hochhuth's dramatic practice at this point. Its inclusion in or omission from a performance of the play can therefore change the impact of the drama substantially. The most important feature of the frame, which distinguishes it from the play-within-the-play, is Hochhuth's approach to the dramatis personae. Hochhuth uses a central figure, Dorland, who is individualized but not entirely realistic, and surrounds him with other figures who are presented as mere types: "an actor," "a West German colonel," "a Japanese professor," "a policeman," "the ghost of an air marshal of Bomber Command," etc. (S, 11). The fictional central figure was supposedly a bomber pilot during World War II, who had participated in the destruction of Dresden. He is the only character who has the same identity in both the frame and the play-within-the-play. His sudden appearance in the third act, in conversation with Bishop Bell, serves as a kind of flashback. Dorland is now an activist working for the creation of an international convention to limit air warfare. For the occasion of the one hundredth anniversary of the Geneva convention in 1964, he has written a drama about the bombing, which is to be performed in the ruins of Coventry Cathedral. It is clear that Hochhuth identified with this author of the play-within-the-play.

Dorland's view of the theater is similar to that of his creator. Thus he indicates in the frame that he too thinks of the theater as a "moralische Anstalt," that he intends his play not just to stir up historical controversy about Churchill, but to agitate in favor of legislation to prevent the bombing of civilians. Here the link to the Vietnam War is made explicit (S, 50). Dorland, speaking for Hochhuth, demonstrates that the latter did not intend his play as an historical drama, but rather as a *Diskussionsstück* (discussion play), so as to teach a lesson for present action.

Dorland makes this transition between past and present most evident by the way in which he himself moves from one time level to the other. He is able to move easily in time and place because Hochhuth conceived him as a mythical, allegorical figure. He borrowed the name Dorland from the supposed author of the medieval *Everyman* (S, 14). Here he represents every soldier, every pilot; his personal feelings of guilt for the death of countless innocent women and children suggest the possibility that all soldiers might be guilty of such crimes. It is Dorland's role in both the frame and the play-within-the-play that reflects the general reference to "soldiers" in the title. In *The Deputy,* Hochhuth had treated the doctor in a similar fashion, but here the use of allegory is more justified and more effective, since this figure is formally set apart from the rest of the characters, providing a frame of reference for under-standing the Churchill action.

Throughout the frame Dorland is engaged in a series of discussions, primarily with acquaintances out of his past. This imaginary dialogue with memory figures is what Hochhuth called a "trial of conscience" (*Gewissensprozeß*), a kind of self-accusation in monologue form (S, 15). Dorland, now faced with a fatal illness, introduces all the major arguments that will be used in the play-within-the-play by means of this personal inventory in which he tries to atone for his guilt. Hochhuth unfortunately did not entirely trust the ability of the audience to move freely with the mystery play character from one vision to another, so he returns him constantly to the present reality level, in which he engages in discussion with a sculptor who is working on a statue for the new Coventry Cathedral or directs the actors where to go for the dress rehearsal.

Within the framework, Hochhuth also departs from his previous practice by projecting a photograph — a device he had consciously avoided in *The Deputy*. It is the picture of a dead woman who haunts Dorland's memory and thus, for him, becomes the figure of death itself (S, 26). He had seen the woman while being forced to dig graves after having had to bail out over Dresden. Her eye sockets are burned out, but inexplicably her hair remains. The projection was to be used twice during the opening framework sequence. The importance which Hochhuth attached to it is indicated by the fact that he included the photograph in the published text.[22] By using this device, Hochhuth was able to overcome some of the difficulties he had faced in *The Deputy* in trying to present Auschwitz on stage with traditional stage sets, for this single document symbolically suggests something of the horror of the bombing, which, like the concentration camps, defied portrayal in ordinary dramatic terms. Yet this one picture was an exception. Hochhuth was still quite far from the extensive use of projection and film techniques that had characterized Piscator's political revues in the 1920s.

In the frame of *Soldiers* Hochhuth also relied on some techniques that remind us of the satirical sketch form developed in political cabarets and that represent another departure from the rather traditional form of *The Deputy*. The first of these individual "numbers," which could be performed by itself consists of a supposed press conference by a former Nazi officer, Colonel Wein-müller, who now has a NATO post and has been invited to attend the London Red Cross conference. He suggests to his audience that they should "approach the question of the responsibility of the individual in a technological war in a spirit of the highest humanistic detachment" (S, 31). Using quotations from the West German writer Reinhard Baumgart, he reveals that his support of the so-called "pre-emptive strike" is based on a *Weltanschauung* which no longer considers the individual as autonomous, but "invisible" and "insignificant" (S, 31). History cannot be viewed as a process guided by individual decisionmakers: "The concepts of guilt and innocence sound like rules of behavior from the nursery — literature should be ashamed to go on churning them out."[23] In fact, Hochhuth was continuing here, within the drama itself, his controversy with Adorno and others. Thus the framework of the play not only introduces the content of the play within the play, but also defends its form, in particular its continued reliance on traditional dramatis personae locked in a conflict of ideas.

In another scene within the frame, Hochhuth himself acknowledged the nature of these individual satirical sketches. The facts were taken from newspapers, he said, and only the form was cabaret ("Kabarett ist nur die Form") (So, 40).[24] Here two delegates to the convention, a drunken American and a drunken Russian, engage in a friendly controversy. This is one place where Vietnam is specifically mentioned (S, 50), but Hochhuth tried to take a position apart from the conflicting ideologies. He has the Russian state his view this way: "Under capitalism man exploits his fellow men, under communism it is other way around" (S, 49).

The way in which Hochhuth intended the framework to raise the issues from an historical to a universal or symbolic level is especially evident in the memory sequence in which Dorland argues with his son. The father concentrates on the similarity between what he did over Dresden and what his son would be willing to do as a NATO pilot. The son considers himself to be an accessory. As a soldier he will not question the kind of strategy that he is being asked to carry out. "Father, it isn't a soldier's business to discuss the technique of war—." But Dorland counters vehemently: "A soldier is a man who fights other soldiers; a pilot who aims at tanks, bridges, factories, dams. That is not you — as it was not me over Dresden" (S, 36–37). Dorland, like Hochhuth, has a cyclical view of history. He thinks of himself and of his son as professional criminals, but he does not extend the parallel from the pilots to the political leaders. Hochhuth, on the other hand, felt sure that leaders still have potentially devastating decisionmaking powers. The power available to the President of the United States after the Gulf of Tonkin resolution was certainly comparable to that of Churchill during World War II. The implications for the present are clearly demonstrable in the historical play-within-the-play. But Hochhuth added the frame in order to show more clearly than in *The Deputy* that his interest in the past was determined by the need to teach a moral lesson for today, rather than to advance an histori-cal thesis in dramatic form.

The opening frame culminates in the appearance of the ghost of Harris, Dorland's former superior officer, who had been in charge of the British bomber command during the war. In addition to reiterating the central issue of the play, Dorland also raises the question here of using the theater as a means to educate the public concerning these problems. The following statement is important for an understanding of the significance of *Soldiers* in the develop-ment of Hochhuth's view of political theater. When Harris suggests that Dorland would have done better to write a play about Francis Drake or Richard the Lion-hearted the theatrical director replies:

> Sir Arthur, the theater isn't a museum.
> History only ceases to be academic
> when it can illustrate for *us* and *now*
> man's inhumanity to man — the historical cliché.
> Richard Coeur de Lion — just a handsome suit of armor,
> no longer alive and no longer dangerous,
> but what you and I did twenty years ago,
> has become the A B C of the airmen of *today.* (S, 55)

The repetition of the word *heute (now, today)* and the stress which Hochhuth put on it, demonstrates without a doubt that he was not so much interested in history for its own sake, as for what it could show the audience about the origins of contemporary military strategy.

The implications that the past had for the present and the future are once again underlined in the final lyrical monologue with which Dorland concludes this vision. As the passage is spoken, the projec-tion of the dead woman of Dresden reappears behind him. But despite this constant reminder of his past, the perspective is turned inexorably toward the present, to the "inheritance" that has been bequeathed on a new generation of generals, pilots, and civilians. In the long stage note that follows, Hochhuth indicated that he did not want the time and place dimensions of the frame to be forgotten while the play-within-the-play was being performed. The stage set of the framework was to indicate the outline of the destroyed Coventry Cathedral. The walls could remain visible on either side of the stage during the subsequent three acts, and the banner that hung over the frame indicating the Red Cross anniversary (1864–1964) would also remind the audience of today (S, 58). Dorland's reappearance in the third act also reinforces this sense of "alienation." Hochhuth praised the London production, in which Dorland acted the part of Bishop Bell in Act III and his son took over *his* role, thus referring back to the father-son conflict in the frame (Dr, 292).[25] Although Hochhuth had previously rejected the Brechtian concept of "alienation," and although his play-within-the-play uses a traditional three act form, the framework of *Soldiers* did introduce several new aspects to his dramatic practice which could only increase the sense of distance on the part of the audience.

The epilogue of the play brings the father and son together once again and is needed to close the framework. Because it is so short, some productions eliminated the epilogue entirely, leaving the audience uncertain as to whether the play was over. Here Hochhuth makes an additional reference to Vietnam. Still, *Soldiers* could hardly qualify as a "Vietnam play," of which there were several at that time, among them Peter Weiss' *Vietnam Diskurs* (1967).[26] But it is clear that Hochhuth did not wish to use the drama to take sides as Weiss was to do. He refused to embrace an ideological position, but argued instead that as long as there was any kind of modern air warfare that involved the bombing of civilians the issues raised in *Soldiers* would be relevant. Thus, by means of his second drama, Hochhuth reconfirmed his belief in his ability to study and distill the "truth" from history. He expanded his belief in the efficacy of the theater as a moral and politically educational institution, and he continued to defend the role of the individual both in the real world and in the drama. But slowly he began to transform the structure of his drama. The ambiguities suggested by both the content and form of *Soldiers* reveal a movement away from the past to the present and future, a movement away from a strictly realistic use of character, time, and place. The resulting work of art is a unique combination of "documentary" historical drama and medieval mystery play, a tragedy of ideas in the classical sense and a modern discussion play with polemical overtones.

## III   *The Aftermath*

Although the reaction to *Soldiers* was equally explosive, it was not as far-reaching or as penetrating as in the case of *The Deputy*. The play was eventually translated into ten languages and had thirty-seven different productions in eleven countries, but the greatest stir was aroused in Britain. The director and the *Dramaturg* (dramatic producer) of the British National Theatre (Sir Laurence Olivier and Kenneth Tynan) had read the play in manuscript form and wanted to produce it. But the Lord Chamberlain refused to grant a license unless permission was obtained in writing from all the surviving relatives of all the hsitorical characters. Despite Olivier's and Tynan's energetic protests, the advisory board of the National Theater accepted this ruling, and the play was effectively banned in Britain. Hochhuth was still able to include this fact in the text before publication. Thus, Dorland announces to his son at the end of the epilogue, that the play has been banned in England (S, 255).

Expectations of a sensation were already running high in Germany at the time of the premiere in October 1967. Hochhuth helped to contribute to the prepremiere publicity by publishing his controversial findings about the mysterious circumstances of Sikorski's death and excerpts from the second act in *Der Spiegel*.[27] But even in this article the playwright was careful to stress that he had written for the stage, for at the beginning he gave his definition of tragedy: "Tragedies have as prerequisites, first, that each of the opponents is right; second, that each cannot give up his just cause. The conflict can only be ended violently, one of the bearers of justice must be destroyed. . . ."[28]

Critics seemed to ignore, for the most part, this acknowledgement that both Churchill and Sikorski had been right. Instead, much of the press argued that Hochhuth was trying to vilify Churchill as he had Pope Pius XII. He was also accused of trying to draw attention away from the guilt of the Germans by shifting the focus to the "other side." A certain animosity characterized the reception of the play in Berlin. Hochhuth was called the "nemesis of Gütersloh," a "pamphletist," and a "national psychiatrist" — even a Nazi.[29] He was bombarded with questions by over one hundred journalists at a press conference held on the day of the premiere, where he was supported by Kenneth Tynan, David Irving, and Ledig-Rowohlt, as well as by the play's director, Hans Schweikart. The German press in particular seemed to delight in registering at least a theatrical defeat the next morning.[30]

Schweikart had been forced to cut the play almost in half, in order to reduce it to a reasonable playing time of three hours, but the cutting had been poorly done. The awkward love plot — which added nothing essential to the drama — was left nearly intact, while the prologue had been emasculated and the epilogue eliminated entirely. The audience was not even sure the play was over at the end of the third act of the play-within-the-play because the frame had been awkwardly left open.[31] The actor, O. E. Hasse, was criticized almost universally for his humorous, sentimental portrayal of Churchill.[32] But most critics concentrated on the audacity of Hochhuth, who had dared, in their view, to air the dirty laundry of the Allies in public by introducing the Sikorski subplot. Boos were heard at the close of the first performance.

Hochhuth once again found it necessary to defend the "truth" he had found in history, as well as the way in which he had dramatized it. In an essay, "Gegen die 'Neue Zürcher Zeitung,'" he countered the argument that he had wished to divert guilt from the Germans by noting that he had been the first dramatist to place Auschwitz on the stage. He had also mentioned the concentration camps in *Soldiers,* along with the demolition raids on Rotterdam and Belgrade (K, 214). He reiterated that the play was not intended to portray Churchill as a criminal, but to suggest the tragic entanglement of a great man. In addition, the play was not so much concerned with that particular historical moment as with the need to limit air warfare today (K, 215–16).

This article is particularly important because it reveals most clearly the ambiguity in Hochhuth's attitude toward the use of history in drama, which had led to the structural dilemma within the play itself. Some critics had suggested that Hochhuth's view of history was similar to that of Lessing. He studied it until he found a pregnant moment that could become the kernel of a dramatic truth.

Despite the historical authenticity of some of the characters, they too were only dramatis personae, and only their function as such could be a legitimate object of criticism.[33] But Hochhuth tried to correct this impression. His drama was not strictly fictional, he stated, and he had not tried to hide behind literary excuses when asked to defend his historical theses. But the distinctions which Hochhuth tried to draw here are very fine indeed. "If, as Lessing wrote, the poet is master of history — I have always felt myself to be its servant. And even the great must pay the price for that: the more slavishly one allows the facts of history to have a say in the work of art, the more annoyedly must one sigh with Schiller: 'My love of history has ruined much of the poetic power in me'" (K, 193).[34]

Hochhuth recognized, however, that in *Soldiers,* as in *The Deputy,* he had been caught between his desire to give history idealistic transparency and his need to adhere to what he felt was the historical truth. He cites Schiller's *Jungfrau von Orleans (The Maid of Orleans)* as an example of a play in which the arbitrary treatment of history had harmed the literary quality of the work — Schiller had Joan die gloriously on the battlefield rather than at the stake — (K, 193–94). But despite Hochhuth's insistence on the need to adhere to the truth of the events, he still refused to have *Soldiers* called a "documentary drama."

> When I reject the label "documentary theater," it is because, unlike the authors of *The Investigation* or *In the Case of Robert Oppenheimer,* I cannot as author ignore the warning of Thomas Mann, which has for me become an aesthetic law: "Without the transparency of the imagination, all material is boring." This assertion leaves room for fantasy even in the historical drama — it permits, for example, what the 'purely' documentary play would exclude, namely, the creation of characters and the transfer of historical happenings to other locales.... But the antithesis of art and truth, which are synonymous, is not nature nor fantasy but arbitrariness. (K, 194–95)

Although Hochhuth thus took great pains to differentiate his theater from the so-called "documentary dramas" written by Kipphardt and Weiss, it should be noted that their position was not so different from his. Despite his adherence to a Marxist ideology and his affirmation of the term "documentary," Weiss also saw the need for the work of art to transcend the level of "pure" documentation. And although *The Investigation* had been largely an exercise in selection and arrangement of documentary material heightened by language, rather than the creation of imaginary figures, in his *Gesang vom Lusitanischen Popanz* (*Song of the Lusitanian Bogey,* 1966), Weiss had clearly departed from "pure" documentation. He used some of the same "cabaret" techniques that Hochhuth had relied on in the framework of *Soldiers.*[35] Yet Hochhuth was certainly correct in stating that both Kipphardt and Weiss had greater faith in the documents. He himself — although he diligently gathered documentary evidence as background material for his plays — was more interested in the eloquent silences of history than in the testimony of trials. *The Deputy* had registered one such silence. And Hochhuth argued that "the things about which one is silent are most often more informative than those about which one speaks" (K, 211). He also explained that the sheer lack of information about Sikorski's death, rather than the wealth of documentary evidence, suggested Churchill's possible involvement. He made the same point in the play itself when he asked: "Do the documents merit closer attention than the gaps? The relation of the document, if one may believe it, to the fact is that of the fragment to the whole vase" (S, 124).

Hochhuth could not remain silent in the ensuing historical and literary debate, which resembled in its thrust, if not its intensity, the discussions that had followed *The Deputy.* Some said it was not the role of the literary critic to ask whether Hochhuth's Sikorski affidavit was valid, while others dealt exclusively with this issue.[36] Some praised Hochhuth's choice of subject matter while attacking his use of form and language. Still others felt that this second play was better than *The Deputy* because it was structurally more sound and less polemical.[37]

It soon became evident that the lack of success of the Berlin production would not put an end to Hochhuth as dramatist or moralist, as some of his most ardent critics had hoped. The English-speaking world was understandably still very interested in the play, and the first English language performance, in Toronto in March 1968, revived interest in it around the world. Clifford Williams, who had staged *The Deputy* in London, was the director, and his handling of the script was more successful than Schweikart's had been. The actor John Colicos, who looked like Churchill, was also credited for the success of this production, as was the translator, Robert David MacDonald (Dr, 478-79). One critic went so far as to call it the most important theater event of the year, hailing Hochhuth as the most important young dramatist in the world.[38] A New York opening of the same production received mixed reviews some months later.[39]

The high point, however, came when the play finally opened in London on December 12, 1968, at the New Theatre, again under the direction of Williams, with John Colicos in the lead. Only the abolition of the Lord Chamberlain's power of theater censorship in September of that year had made this production possible.[40] In order to further reduce the playing time to two hours, and because of the special interest of the English audience in Churchill, the frame had been deleted. This version totally deemphasized the relation between the content of the play-within-the-play and our present, once again concentrating critical attention on the historical validity of Hochhuth's insinuation. Yet Ludwig Marcuse had effectively argued that just this kind of cut should be made in order to avoid the structural dilemma. It would, he felt, do away with all attempts at alienation provided by the framework, and thus allow the audience to identify with the key figure. "The identification with a dramatic figure does not conform to the demands of the prevailing aesthetic. But only in this way will the audience react politically."[41] Marcuse ignores the possibility that the audience might also identify with the "Everyman" of the frame, Dorland.

By then Hochhuth himself was so embroiled in the controversy with historians and journalists over the Sikorski material that he did not take time to object to this radical cutting of the play and the resulting destruction of its original form and intent. But in articles and interviews he continued to point out the relevance of the play for today, especially for Vietnam.[42] He continued to defend tirelessly his conclusion that Sikorski's death had been no accident and that Churchill's involvement was quite feasible. He also argued that he had every right to protect his secret source. David Irving's book had been totally revised and had appeared in German under the less imaginative title, *Moskaus Staatsräson? Sikorski und Churchill — eine tragische Allianz,* in 1969. And in the meantime an unlikely Don Quixote, the actor Carlos Thompson, who had at first befriended Hochhuth and Irving, set out to disprove their thesis. In his rather remarkable book, *The Assassination of Winston Churchill,* he argued that the plane crash had been an accident; but he also tried to damage Hochhuth's reputation in a series of articles and interviews.[43]

The young playwright, a shy and private man, did not entirely relish all this publicity. He once again talked of writing a comedy: "I have no desire to always dirty my hands with these kinds of themes."[44] The discomfiture he felt is best revealed in his account of an imaginary press conference to be held at the wax museum of Madame Tussaud in London. In this "Impromptu de Madame Tussaud," as the story is entitled, the anxious author discusses his hopes and fears with his fatherly publisher, referred to here simply as Ledig. An amused Churchill appears, annoyed at the censorship that had been imposed on *Soldiers:* "Now Whitehall won't even let me make a comeback as a dramatic figure" (H, 67). But, more importantly, this fictional dialogue reveals Hochhuth's thoughts on possible future dramatic topics. While discussing the Kennedy assassination and the murder of Oswald, Hochhuth seems to be contemplating a drama which will show "the outbreak of a fascist era in America" (H, 58). But the playwright is still reluctant to deal with the present directly. "I believe that what happens today cannot yet be portrayed today, but only tomorrow. In dreams everything becomes present, but one cannot dream of the present and therefore one cannot write about it" (H, 58–59).

Once again Hochhuth demonstrated that his intention in *Soldiers* was to use the past as a lesson for the present, when he says of World War II: "Its figures are history — [but] its barbarities are real today, especially the air war against civilians. That is entirely present — nevertheless one can already dream of Churchill!" (H, 59). Thus, while apparently continuing to dream of the past, Hochhuth had already turned his chief attention to the present and future. While critics still argued about his interpretation of historical events, Hochhuth was busy articulating his political views in a variety of essays, so as to speak to our present problems. I must therefore agree with the provost of Coventry, H. C. N. Williams, who stated in his introduction to *Soldiers* that "Rolf Hochhuth's plays are not to be judged by the particular historical context within which he has written them. They are to be judged by a perspective of the never-ending tragedy of the history of the betrayal of human hope."[45] In the perspective of Hochhuth's cyclical view of history the present and future are revealed by the past. And as the tragedy of history is never-ending, so too is the task of the dramatist and moralist Hochhuth.

## CHAPTER 4

# The Artist and Politics:
# Letters, Essays, Speeches

## I  *The Citizen-Author*

H OCHHUTH'S letter to President Lübke written in 1964 demonstrated that this engaged German author was willing to go beyond the strictly literary form of the drama in order to make his political views known. Yet this was not a result of frustration with the theater as a vehicle for political expression. Instead, Hochhuth considered such position statements an integral part of his artistic activity. Unlike his contemporary, Peter Weiss, for whom the apparent disparity between his desire for political activity and his role as an author had created a deep personal conflict, Hochhuth remained realistic and uncomplicated in this regard.[1] He had tried from the beginning of his career to be consistent politically, both as an author and as a citizen, and he did not view these two roles as conflicting. He made his position very clear in an article entitled "Über Zuständigkeit von Nicht-Fachleuten" ("Concerning the Competence of Non-Specialists," [K, 60–64]). Here he defended his right to take stands on political issues in his dramas as well as in letters, essays, and speeches.

Hochhuth had been severely criticized not only for his historical studies in conjunction with the first two plays, but even more bitterly, at least in Germany, for a political essay entitled "Der Klassenkampf ist nicht zu Ende" ("The class struggle is not yet over"), which had first appeared in *Der Spiegel* in 1965.[2] Hochhuth was particularly sensitive to the frequent accusation that he was a dilettante ("Hochhuth as economist, Hochhuth as historian" [K, 63]). He rejected such criticism, however, calling it part of a long German tradition based on the misconception that poetics and politics do not mix. Up to this point, however, Hochhuth had differentiated carefully between his roles as dramatist and citizen. In *The Deputy,* the "Historical Sidelights" were carefully set apart from the rest of the play. In *Soldiers,* as we have seen, although the separation was not as pronounced, the question of the bombing of civilian centers was left open to discussion, whereas Hochhuth took a firm stand on the issue in the Lübke letter.

Nevertheless, the two spheres of activity had always been intertwined. Hochhuth considered himself a citizen-author. He felt that truth in the one area was impossible to achieve without truthfulness and honesty in the other. "An author does not have to write politically in order to tell the truth — but he cannot write the truth, even as an unpolitical author, if he is — as a citizen — the accomplice of liars" (K, 61). Thus for Hochhuth good citizenship was an important prerequisite for good authorship, whether the author was politically engaged or not. For this reason, his essays, letters, and speeches must be considered an integral, although lesser, part of his *oeuvre,* since it is only through them that one can arrive at a clear understanding of his development as an engaged author. Hochhuth often elucidated political ideas in his essays that were later incorporated into his dramas. Especially during the period after *Soldiers,* the ideas first worked out in speeches, essays, and letters formed the basis for eventual shifts in his dramatic practice. It is therefore more fruitful to consider them as a group at this juncture, rather than strictly chronologically along with the dramas.

Hochhuth elaborated his concept of the citizen-author in an open letter to the Czech writer Ladislav Mňačko in 1964. Mňačko had appealed to Hochhuth after the piracy of his work, *Verspätete Reportagen (Delayed Reports),* by a West German publisher (K, 87). Hochhuth used the opportunity of a reply to clarify his views on the relationship between the engaged author and party politics. Unlike Mnacko, who was a communist party member, and unlike Weiss, who had eventually resolved his conflict by embracing Marxist ideology, he insisted on the need to be free of ties to party or ideology of any kind. Even when a work like Mňačko's *Reportagen* was critical of the party in question, Hochhuth rejected the very solidarity that it implied. He wished to point out, however, that he was not specifically anticommunist, for he insisted on the need for viable communist parties in countries like the United States, but he resisted any one party system because the adherence to any party line could not ultimately lead to the truth. "And partisanship [*Parteilichkeit*] — taken literally — cannot represent truth, but only a partial truth, and for that reason the concepts of unity [*Vereinigung*] and centralization [*Einheitlichkeit*], which are so very easily accepted, are in no way desirable if they do away with conflict-producing dialogue. History proves that" (K, 93).

Typically, Hochhuth relies on history as the ultimate source of truth. He maintained in the letter that Stalinism and Nazism were not unexplainable aberrations, but the clearest modern examples of the ultimate consequence of "absolutizing an ideological program" (K, 87). More important for an understanding of the relationship between Hochhuth's rejection of ideology and his concept of drama is the need expressed here to preserve conflict-producing dialogue. At this point in his development Hochhuth still considered dialogue to be the natural prerequisite for the drama, but in his view there could be no real dialogue and no dramatic tension if there was no room for the clash of political ideas.

If neither ideology nor party can provide the engaged author Hochhuth with a clear guide to action, of what does his engagement consist? Hochhuth himself explained it in the exchange with Mňačko by saying that the writer must remain true not to party or ideology but to his own "personal problematic" (K, 97). For Hochhuth this "problematic" is expressed as a capacity for recognizing wrong in the world and experiencing a consequent sense of moral outrage. In effect, the individual moral sense of the author himself is posited as an absolute in place of party or ideology. Hochhuth insisted that one must remain true to this personal moral sense, "even if it forces one to make statements that are completely useless, or endanger youth, or are subversive, or even asocial, to the point of being criminal, and whose entire sense is only their truth" (K, 97–98).

Thus Hochhuth's search for truth is inner-directed. As citizen-author he has never expressed solidarity with a group, a church or a political party, nor has he found it necessary, as did Peter Weiss, to support his political views ideologically. Instead he has continued, throughout the 1960s and 1970s, to orient himself according to his own personal compass, a moral "true North" that he has held within himself. Politically he followed this personal indicator by making both theoretical and issue-oriented statements. Dramatically this pathfinder oriented him after *The Deputy* and *Soldiers* toward the portrayal of the conflict of ideas in the present rather than the historical past. But it was the political essays written between 1964 and 1970 that prepared the way for this and other changes in his dramatic practice.

## II   *Hochhuth and the Federal Republic of Germany:* War and Class War

Despite the move to Switzerland in 1963, Hochhuth's spiritual homeland remains the Federal Republic of Germany, and this country bore the brunt of the attack made in his first controversial political essay, "Der Klassenkampf ist nicht zu Ende." Despite his use of the term "class struggle" in the title, Hochhuth was not referring to an international ideological conflict, but to specific economic issues within the Federal Republic. In this respect he also differs from Peter Weiss, whose political pamphlets of the same period dealt with the issue of capitalism versus socialism on an exclusively international level.[3] But Hochhuth took direct aim at Bonn. Thus, while his dramas had attracted a world audience, the controversy over this position statement, although furious, was limited almost entirely to those in the Federal Republic of Germany who found themselves under fire.

According to Hochhuth, class struggle is not yet over in West Germany because there is still an unjust distribution of wealth. The middle class citizen, who makes up the majority, is lulled into believing that he is not really disadvantaged because he is readily able to purchase consumer goods, while those who suffer extreme poverty in West German cities have no such illusions (K, 23). Hochhuth blames all the political parties in Bonn for contributing to the continuance of this inequity, yet he pictures the government as powerless in the face of the lobbies of large industry and the trusts, like Axel Springer's press monopoly (K, 27). He lashes out in particular at those politicians and intellectuals who refuse to recognize the tensions that still exist in West German society, once again taking specific aim at Theodor Adorno (K, 30, 44). While giving a pessimistic picture of the present, Hochhuth warns that some day there will be a great awakening, when the "economic miracle" will be over and the West German economy will take a downward turn, when the people will be faced with unemployment and inflation again; then they will realize that they have been duped by expressions like *Sozialpartnerschaft* (social partnership). The people will become radicalized and will sweep away the last vestiges of democracy by means of terror (K, 28–29).

Although Hochhuth thus pictured the possibility of a future revolution in West Germany — if political alternatives were not found — he was not at this point advocating revolution but trying to suggest what could be done to prevent such an eventuality. He called for strikes by workers and suggested that the then head of IG-Metall, Otto Brenner, be brought to Bonn as *Sozialminister* (minister of social affairs). Although he himself could not entirely accept Brenner's program for public ownership of the key industires and the participation by workers in the administration of factories (*Mitbestimmung*), Hochhuth pictured him as a kind of savior, as the only man who could lend protection to the needy, knowing full well that this man was anathema to both the Christian Democratic (CDU) and Social Democratic (SPD) parties (K, 43–44).

It is typical for Hochhuth that in trying to offer a practical solution to what he considered to be an economic but also a moral problem, he searched for an individual leader (K, 48). In fact, his whole vision of the economic and social ills is an extension of his campaign on behalf of the individual. Above all he was concerned with what happens to the individual in a society based on property, fearing that the person would lose any sense of his relevancy in the face of larger economic and political forces unless each human being could be assured of having real capital. "The way our world is arranged, freedom for the individual can only be realized through money, only through property" (K, 48). In an interesting aside, Hochhuth asserts that money can also be the stuff of tragedy (*Tragödienstoff*).

Hochhuth thus was not rejecting the capitalist economic system in favor of a purely socialist one. He made it very clear, for example, that he believed that the people in the German Democratic Republic had as little real property as those in the Federal Republic, only in the East it was the state rather than private industry which controlled it (K, 34). Hochhuth in fact was simply proposing a redistribution of wealth (*Besitzverteilung*) within the present order. Here he was seeking to humanize capitalism, just as he had tried to humanize warfare in the Lübke letter and in *Soldiers*.

The essay "Der Klassenkampf ist nicht zu Ende," however naive

it may be economically and politically, is characterized by Hochhuth's characteristic tone of moral outrage, particularly in those
passages that refer to specific examples of poverty in West Germany. The theme of poverty is one to which Hochhuth would return both as citizen and as author. As an author he intended to
arouse political controversy by his statements, and he did actually
manage to do so, especially because of his polemical style.[4] The
level of the reaction was not always elevated either. Chancellor
Erhard, for instance, simply dismissed Hochhuth as a "Pinscher"
(fox-terrier [K, 18]). *Der Spiegel* found it necessary to distance
itself from the opinions expressed in the article (K, 49–52). Ironically, given Hochhuth's rejection of all the Bonn political parties,
the article was first republished in a collection of essays in support
of the SPD, *Plädoyer für eine neue Regierung oder keine Alternative (Pleading for a new government or no alternative).* But the
importance that Hochhuth attributed to it became apparent when
the article was made the lead study in his volume *Krieg und
Klassenkrieg (War and Class War),* published in 1971. At that time,
the author attached an account of the discussion surrounding the
original publication, denouncing all those who had rejected his
thesis and making personal attacks on politicians Erhard, Willy
Brandt, and Franz Josef Strauß, and on editors Axel Springer and
Rudolf Augstein.[5]

Despite the apparently radical title of the essay and the highly
personal invective of the rebuttals, Hochhuth had little in common
with the so-called "extraparliamentary opposition" which was
active during the 1960s in German universities. In a discussion with
Berlin university students in December 1967, the differences
became quite evident.[6] The students charged Hochhuth with being
a member of the "establishment." He, on the other hand, given his
basically pessimistic *Weltanschauung,* could not share their revolutionary optimism. Nor were they interested in his pleas for human-
izing war or capitalism. It was clear from their discussion that
Hochhuth and the radical students were speaking two different languages, even when they used similar terms, like "class war." This
did not prevent Hochhuth, however, from joining with the students
and other writers like Heinrich Böll in speaking out against the
passage of the *Notstandsgesetze* (emergency laws) on May 28,
1968.[7] But Hochhuth's speech on this occasion only highlighted the
essential differences between his approach and that of the West

German student movement. While lashing out at all the parliamentary parties, especially the Socialists, on the one hand, Hochhuth revealed that he could not support the kind of mass action that characterized student opposition. For him the only hope was reliance on a prominent individual like Brenner, or on an elite group (K, 137). He once again used this opportunity to call on Brenner to unleash a general strike, not shying away from the "personalization of the conflict" because, unlike the students, he felt that acts of state are also personal acts. "'People as individuals are responsible for them and must answer for them'" (K, 140-41).[8]

Although the ideas expressed in his speech against the emergency laws did not represent a significant change over Hochhuth's previous position, this was the first time he went beyond a mere expression of his belief in the power of individual leaders to suggest a strategy for the overthrow of the Bonn government — the infiltration of the parties and unions by a small, trustworthy elite (K, 141). But despite the moderate optimism revealed in this strategy, Hochhuth remained basically pessimistic about the possibilities for radical change in West Germany. He indicated his grave reservations in an answer to a *Spiegel* questionnaire that same year, "Hat die Revolution in der Bundesrepublik eine Chance?" ("Does revolution have a chance in the Federal Republic?" [H, 347-51]).

Hochhuth and others had been asked to respond to a statement by the left-wing author Hans Magnus Enzensberger to the effect that what West Germany must confront is not communism but the possibility of revolution. Enzensberger felt that the political system in West Germany could not be overhauled; one must either accept the status quo or seek to institute a new system of government (H, 347). In his reply, Hochhuth pointed out that it was the sons and daughters of the middle class, not the proletariat, who had been the real element of revolt in West German society during the 1960s. The working class had remained conservative, but the students who called for revolution were hopeless romantics, unwilling to participate in the parliamentary process. Both of these factors reduced their revolt to a "rotes Glasperlenspiel" (H, 349).[9] In his answer to this questionnaire Hochhuth suggested once again that the only way to achieve a transformation in a country like the Federal Republic was from within, through the systematic infiltration of the ruling oligarchy by a small group of "decent" men (H, 348). But for the first time he not only attacked politicians and students, but writers like himself as well. "There is also no revolution in Germany, because there are no intellectuals, carriers of ideas, who are willing to risk their lives or even their jobs. The writer is no exception" (H, 351). The criticism was in part self-directed, for despite all his efforts both at citizenship and authorship, Hochhuth seemed at times to regard his journalistic and dramatic writing as pitifully inadequate vehicles for real political change.

### III   *Hochhuth and the United States of America:*
### *The Development of a Revolutionary Strategy*

In yet another political essay, "Angst vor der 'Schutz'-Macht USA: Ein Rundblick nach der Ermordung Luther Kings und Robert Kennedys" ("Fear of the so-called protective power, USA: An overview after the assassinations of Luther King and Robert Kennedy"), Hochhuth elaborated his theory of infiltration, this time using the United States as an example and repeating his contention that in order to bring about radical changes in a capitalist society, one must look to revolutionary individuals who are already members of the ruling elite. This kind of revolutionary will be a member of the oligarchy created by the military-industrial complex, but he will have the interests of the people at heart. Hochhuth further explained why such infiltration by an elite was necessary, especially in the United States, and why one could not rely on the working class to carry out the revolution. Economic factors alone, he insisted, do not create class consciousness, and there has never been a viable workers party in the United States, for the workers there are among the most conservative forces (K, 146).

Despite the fact that in this essay Hochhuth was writing primarily about the USA, he could not forget the relationship between that country and the Federal Republic of Germany. He depicted the latter as an economic satellite of the US-Goliath, which was proving to be a dangerous "protective power." He criticized Konrad Adenauer, therefore, for having allowed West Germany to become a "colony" of America, and accused him, as well as Walter Ulbricht in the East, for having placed ideology above nation, thus perpetuating the division of Germany in the postwar period (K, 154). Hochhuth felt West Germany was moving inevitably in the same direction as the United States, that is, toward the establishment of a plutocratic oligarchy under the guise of democracy.

Hochhuth was primarily interested in outlining a revolutionary strategy, however, and in doing so he applied a method that he would also use in his next drama, *Guerillas* — looking to the recent American past for clues to the future. He felt that Vietnam had again demonstrated that capitalism cannot function without resort to a wartime economy (K, 167-68). The deaths of John and Robert Kennedy and Martin Luther King were evidence that change in America would not be possible without resort to violence. Whether or not a transformation of the social structure in that country could be achieved even with force remained uncertain (K, 175). Nevertheless, Hochhuth's ultimate prediction for the future of the USA was either a "coup" from the left or civil war. There was no doubt in his mind that the first option was preferable.

Between the time that "Angst vor der 'Schutz'-Macht USA" was first published in *konkret* in 1968 and the appearance of Hochhuth's next drama in 1970, which put his ideas about a future American revolution into dramatic form, the author's position with regard to this infiltration strategy remained basically the same. But only the play, which was severely attacked by critics, brought his thesis widespread public attention. On the defensive, he tried to marshal further evidence in support of his theory in an article entitled "Keine Revolution ohne Infiltration" ("No revolution without infiltration" [K, 217-47]). But this article hardly referred to the drama, concentrating instead on a reiteration and clarification of the author's political views, for he felt that they must first be understood so that his drama could be.

Hochhuth had not changed his basic idea. He stated it firmly once again: "The way to power — when no war forces a change of regime — is by means of infiltration into the palace, the police, the bureaucracy, and above all, the army" (K, 223). He insisted that such an infiltration strategy must be supported by the military, for no revolution is possible without its cooperation. But the military will always be nationalistic, so he foresaw many individual, national revolutions, rather than an international movement (K, 226). Hochhuth admitted, however, that one could not guarantee what would follow such a coup, since it was the individual military dictator who would determine what became of the nation. Hochhuth thus returned to his central theme of the role of the individual leader. He criticized his opponents for overlooking that role, especially those orthodox Marxists who could not accept that the proletariat had not, and would not, bring about the revolution, who let their ideology get in the way of the "truth of history": "'The coup d'état was the vehicle of the Bolshevik revolution and Lenin was its first and most talented technician'" (K, 228).[10]

It is important to note that, despite his rejection of ideology, Hochhuth was particularly concerned that his critics understand that even Marx would have supported his contention that history is an interaction between the fateful workings of political and economic forces and the free will of individuals. "Even Marx allowed the individual freedom of action within the framework of historical necessity — not handcuffed by it —" (K, 242–43). Thus Hochhuth blamed only the dogmatic tradition of Marxism for not recognizing what he saw as the humanistic core of Marxist thought.

Yet despite Hochhuth's expressed concern for the individual and the importance he placed in the active role of certain individuals within an already existing elite, he had slightly modified his approach, especially his attitude toward the use of the general strike. Whereas in "Klassenkampf" and in the speech against the emergency laws Hochhuth had advocated the strike, here he suggested that although it could cause temporary harm to the government, in the final analysis the civilian population suffered more from it. A coup, on the other hand, was less likely, he felt, to disrupt the daily lives of the populace. Hochhuth was hard pressed to find historical examples, relying heavily in this respect on the work of a young British historian, Edward Luttwak. He cites Peru and Bolivia as two countries in which socialist regimes had been safely introduced by revolutionary coups, further proof that it was a politically and ideologically "value-free" (*wertfreies*) vehicle to gain power (K, 223) — that it need not necessarily come from the right. Even with this typical search for historical models on Hochhuth's part, he did not lose sight of the present. Although in both his previous essays and the drama, *Guerillas*, he had focused specifically on the United States as a country ripe for such a coup from the left, he reminded his readers that the attack could not be one-sided: "In both centers of power the oligarchies — the spiritual one in Moscow, the plutocratic one in Washington — should be replaced by force with a republic" (K, 244).

It is only at the close of the article, however, that Hochhuth suggests that the outcome of the revolutions he envisaged should be humanistic, socialistic republics. None of his descriptions of military dictatorships give us any indication of how these republics are to be established, nor how the redistribution of wealth is to be carried out. And his own confidence that such military regimes need not be fascist in character is hardly reassuring. What is readily apparent, however, is that Hochhuth, while covering new ground in his political essays, letters, and speeches, returned again and again to the central issue of the individual in contemporary society. Behind the political and economic issues lurked the unforgotten concern for the role of the individual with its aesthetic implications. Since Hochhuth's approach to this role had in fact changed so little since 1963, his essay "Soll das Theater die heutige Welt darstellen?" which had outlined his position on the subject, was twice republished, eliciting a belated, but important response from his chief antagonist Adorno.

## IV *The Individual versus Mass Man: The Adorno Controversy*

In the "Klassenkampf" essay of 1965, Hochhuth had restated the cause of the individual as follows: "But humanity exists solely where man is still, or once again, regarded as an individual, not as a member of a group. One belongs to the masses oneself, or there is no such thing. There is a mass of [a lot of] money but no mass of people and no mass men" (K, 44).[11] It is hardly surprising that in the very same paragraph Hochhuth took aim once again at Adorno for having contributed, in his opinion, to the myth that the individual is no longer a meaningful category. But when Adorno replied in an open letter to the *Frankfurter Allgemeine Zeitung* in February 1967, it was not to this more recent personal attack, but to the 1963 essay "Soll das Theater die heutige Welt darstellen?" Hochhuth's initial statement of aesthetic purpose had finally come to the philosopher's attention because of its inclusion in a *Festschrift* for Georg Lukács in 1966. Adorno felt that his ideas had been distorted and that he himself had been misunderstood.[12] The open letter was an attempt to clarify his position, but it only demonstrated that the differences between himself and Hochhuth were not based on misunderstandings, but on their differing views of the world and man's role in it.

At the center of the controversy was the question of the portrayal of the absurd. While Adorno admitted that Hochhuth might be

correct in stating that the reality of history included the absurd element, he argued that the traditional dramaturgy of the kind that
Hochhuth had advocated in the essay and used in *The Deputy* and
*Soldiers* would not suffice to demonstrate such a convergence. "No
traditional dramaturgy with major characters can reproduce it. The
absurdity of the real demands a form that destroys the realistic approach."[13] For Hochhuth, however, the only possible dramatic
form was the realistic portrayal of conflict between individual
human beings, especially those in decisionmaking positions. He
had not changed his position on this important formal question
since he had first answered the *Theater heute* questionnaire. "Decisions in drama require the personalization of conflicts; that is still
true even if popular-Marxists [*Vulgär-Marxisten*] reject it as a
violation of their belief" (H, 318).

Adorno's response proceeded from a brief analysis of modern
society, in which he depicted man — caught in the production
apparatus — as characterized by a radical decline of individualism,
to praise of Absurd literature, which embodies this "correct consciousness" in its form and content. Adorno considered it
"phoney" — he himself uses the American slang expression — to
place individual characters on stage, as if such individuals were still
"subjects." Instead, he praised the drama of Samuel Beckett, because in it the subjects of traditional drama have become
"objects," reflecting the true nature of our world. Adorno com-
plained of Hochhuth's drama: "Everywhere one is personalizing
things, attributing anonymous forces, which the theoretically inex-
perienced person can no longer grasp, and whose hellish coldness
can no longer be tolerated by the anxious consciousness, to living
people in order to save something of spontaneous experience; even
you have not proceeded any differently."[14]

Adorno did note correctly, as I have also pointed out, that Hochhuth's approach to drama floundered when he tried to portray the
fate of the victims of the world's inhumanity. But he rejected
Hochhuth's use of dramatic form, not because it was ineffective in
this respect, but because of a basically different philosophy. Hochhuth had argued that free choice still existed, even if individual
freedom was limited, and he felt that this freedom of the subject
was also essential to preserve dramatic action. But Adorno falsely
accused him of trying to preserve traditional drama at all costs by
avoiding reality, refusing to believe that Hochhuth's perception of

reality could be in fact different from his own. For Adorno the Absurd theater provided the answer to the inevitable death of tragedy, for in it drama did not have freedom of the subject as a prerequisite, but showed the destruction of that freedom. For him Hochhuth's support of the individual was an empty appeal to humanity in an inhuman world. In conclusion, Adorno suggested that the young author should pay closer attention to the inhumanity of man, both past and present. This is certainly an unwarranted criticism, for it was only because of Hochhuth's tremendous concern for the inhumanity of man toward his fellow men that he searched so tirelessly for examples of his basic humanity.

When *Theater heute* republished the Adorno letter in July 1967, a direct response from Hochhuth was promised for the August issue. For whatever reason, it did not appear.[15] It was unusual for Hochhuth to pass up a chance for rebuttal, but his silence should not be construed as either agreement or acquiescence. Perhaps he felt that his position had been fully explained in the original article. And by continuing, in his political essays and in his subsequent dramas, to defend the cause of the individual as subject rather than object, he made his own kind of reply to Adorno's challenge.

In the introduction to *Krieg und Klassenkrieg,* Fritz Raddatz points to the Adorno controversy as embodying the single essential issue in Hochhuth's *oeuvre.* For Hochhuth, he maintained, "people are considered changeable and situations can be influenced by them."[16] Thus the individual can overcome anonymity; he has a face and a name, even within the crowd. It is significant that Raddatz sides with Hochhuth even on the aesthetic issues involved in the controversy. "What is more important, the aesthetic position is also untenable. The theory of the incomprehensible nature of mechanisms, of the impossibility of making them 'perceptual' is a result of just such cognitive innocence. With the help of this agnosticism, a ritual impotence is established, which finally sets up formal postulates that are just never proved."[17] Raddatz is correct in pointing out Adorno's misplaced praise of Brecht's drama, because in this respect the opposition between Hochhuth and Brecht is a false one. Whatever the great differences in form and content, Hochhuth and Brecht do share a common prerequisite of political theater, that is, a belief that the anonymous forces that are at work in our world are both discernible and portrayable.[18] Without this firm belief in the *Durchschaubarkeit* of the world (its ability to be understood) neither author could have begun to translate his understanding of it into dramatic action.

Given Adorno's praise of Brecht's "episodic drama," it is ironic that Hochhuth is actually closer to the philosopher's position than Brecht. For the former's view of the world has always betrayed an underlying pessimism because of his rejection of optimistic ideologies and his appreciation for the absurd element in reality. And nowhere did Hochhuth make this clearer than in the essay "Soll das Theater die heutige Welt darstellen?," for in it he warned that one should be careful not to draw too clear a distinction between his theater of reality and the theater of the Absurd. He called it "nonsense — so common today — to play up the realistic and the absurd as opposites. Our world, so full of the absurd that every day one has an hour when one is in danger of finding it entirely absurd, should supply the theater of the future with an inexhaustible source of theater props and serve as a controlling agent which cannot be ignored, because with every departure from it [reality], the unobligated, unaimed quality [of the theater] increases" (H, 325). From the beginning Hochhuth's search for meaning and his discovery of humanity had been gained only at great cost. Always there had been the moments when he was in danger of relegating everything to the realm of the absurd, giving up the struggle on behalf of the individual. But the Sisyphean effort had to go on, and his internal moral compass continued to point the way.

CHAPTER 5

# Hochhuth's American Revolution

## I  A Methodological Turn Toward the Future

AS early as 1967, Hochhuth had announced a comedy as his next drama, but the political essays pointed him — at least temporarily — in another direction. It was hardly a surprise, after the essay "Angst vor der 'Schutz'-Macht USA," that he chose the United States as the setting for his third drama — subtitled "Tragödie." But significantly, he barely mentioned *Guerillas,* published in 1970, either in this essay that immediately preceded it, or in "Keine Revolution ohne Infiltration," which was ostensibly written as a defense of the drama. He seemed more concerned that his political views, which formed the basis for the dramatic action, be understood, perhaps because he felt most vulnerable to attack on that front. In the *Vorwort* (introduction) to the drama, however, he not only reiterated his political analysis, but also outlined a dramatic theory which — although not entirely new — was modified to coincide with his recently formulated political views. Hochhuth's concept of political drama had to change — if only slightly — in order to accommodate a possibility for political theater of which he was simultaneously proffering an example. The introduction was his first formal statement of an aesthetic position since "Soll das Theater die heutige Welt darstellen?" and, as such, might be considered as an indirect reply to Adorno. Although it did not supersede the previous statement, it explored a new temporal dimension — the future. Even more than the "Historical Sidelights" of *The Deputy,* it provided a key not only to the content of the play in question, but to its form and intent as well.

Typically, Hochhuth started with a consideration of history, for in the drama he still wanted to show the truth through history. First he suggested that historiography was not a science (*Wissenschaft*) at all, but that it was closer to great epic or tragedy, was metaphysical in nature, and should treat the ideal rather than the real. What was needed, he insisted, was the intuitive perception of goals, a search for historical constants that could be used *a priori* for the projection of future events. Hochhuth agreed with Ortega y Gasset, from whom he quoted, that as physics has a metaphysics, history must have a metahistory: "'the concrete is only understandable after a previous abstraction and analysis'" (G, 9). He rejected a method which, he felt, reduced historical writing to *Dokumenten-stapelei* (piling up of documents). It is ideas that must be distilled from the *Dokumentenschutt,* and that can serve the dramatist as a basis for tragic conflict (G, 10).

Hochhuth's current view of history thus allowed for change as well as for an unchanging basic nature: "The reality of history consists at any moment of a number of changeable, but also of a core of unchanging elements" (G, 10). The discovery of these cyclical patterns could, on the one hand, aid in the reconstruction of a concrete epoch in history, but, more importantly, it could lead to the projection of coming events such as a revolution: "To hunt for historical constants, which one culls from the documentary rubble, instead of proceeding inversely, is a method that leads, in the case of the United States, in and of itself to the anticipation of certain events" (G, 10).

For his analysis of the situation in the USA Hochhuth relied on his own personal observations, made during two visits to that country, as well as on the writings of others, in particular H. G. Wells and L. L. Matthias (G, 12).[1] The latter, a historian and sociologist, had become a close personal friend of Hochhuth after the move to Basle, and the young dramatist, grateful for the encouragement received, dedicated *Guerillas* to him.[2] But he also gave credit to Edward Luttwak for convincing him that a coup d'état was the only expedient revolutionary strategy in a country like the United States:

The guerillas practice on stage what Luttwak's famous handbook of coup d'état recommends on the basis of the experience that in the last decade seventy-three coups have been successful in forty-six countries. The coup d'état — as the least bloody revolutionary model, the only one that can prevent the massacre of civil war — is supposed to overturn the plutocratic oligarchy, the club of those one hundred and twenty families to whom "all the rest belong." (G, inside cover)[3]

Once Hochhuth had discovered this particular constant in history — the necessity of a coup d'état — he could reconsider the role of the dramatist. In *The Deputy* and *Soldiers* he had only attempted to reinterpret the past, but now in *Guerillas* he intended to project it into the future:

Thus author is just another word for catalyst, for an author can also trigger accelerated reactions. And if this drama attempts to arouse the audience by means of scenes that depict an incitement to riot — a crime which since 1968 is punishable in the USA by imprisonment — then this intent is also based on a fundamental law of chemistry: a substance reacts chemically in proportion to its concentration; a play concentrates phenomena from the real world and subjects them to ideas, for revolutions need ideas as much as they need guns. (G, 14)

Hochhuth seems to be saying here that his political drama, through its portrayal of the conflict of ideas, could contribute to the future revolution by speeding up the already inevitable process of history. This relative optimism seems to be in stark contrast to a statement he made only a short while later in "Keine Revolution ohne Infiltration," where he disparagingly refers to the writer as "an entertainment-clown who, without risk, can be integrated into society" (K, 236–37).[4] But such a fluctuation between optimism and pessimism had always been characteristic of Hochhuth's *Weltanschauung,* and in the introduction to *Guerillas* he was making the most optimistic assessment to date of the value of the drama as a vehicle for political and social change. Political theater was not dead, he asserted, even though its demise — like that of the novel — was periodically announced (G, 19).

But Hochhuth also reemphasized that *his* political drama was not to be understood as a reconstruction of reality. He remained consistent in his rejection of the term "documentary drama": "This tragedy is neither a historical nor a documentary play. It gives an analysis and sketch of the ideas of a conspiracy, whose preparation in North and South America makes up the fictional plot" (G, inside cover). On the one hand Hochhuth rejected the technique of the newscast, which he felt characterized the street theater of the student movement (G, 20): "The whirl of persons and events in the centrifuge, which presumably one calls history, taken apart and mashed up, may be the technique of the newscast. But a stage that tried to develop a style along those lines would not 'document' much more than its own technical and spatial inadequacy. Newscasts entertain because they accept the common misconception that a photographic slice of reality is realistic'' (G, 19). But, on the other hand, he continued to spurn Brecht's use of the parable and *Verfremdung* (alienation) because it distanced issues to the point that they no longer provoked comparison with everyday reality (G, 18).

Hochhuth thus returned to the central issue of "Realism" that he had first explored in "Soll das Theater die heutige Welt darstellen?" He still believed in 1970 that Realistic devices were essential to the drama, and yet he realized more painfully now — after the criticism to which his first two plays had been subjected — that such Realism must not be confused with Naturalism, i.e., with slavish reproduction. He tried to prevent such misunderstanding in the case of *Guerillas* by explaining that in it reality had been reduced to its symbolic value: "Die Realität [wurde] auf ihren Symbolwert entschlackt" (G, 20). But he had made similar cautionary statements to little avail in *The Deputy*.[5] What is new here is the suggestion that the dramatist should try to achieve in the aesthetic realm what Ortega had outlined as a goal for the historian; that is, to discover in the individual what is typical and to seek his unchanging core, then to move from the general to the particular, rather than the inverse. Hochhuth hoped to prevent misunderstanding of his intent by applying this new method in turning toward the future and away from strictly historical subjects, although a study of history was essential to it.

Hochhuth's new definition of political theater was bound to include his important shift in perspective:

The task of political theater cannot be the *reproduction* of reality — which is political per se — but rather the *projection* of a new conflicting reality. It will only affect the audience and simultaneously preserve its own character as theater when its agitation is moral rather than political, for its role is not that of the politician. It may be legitimate for the film to reproduce history, but it is drama's role, abstractly, to anticipate history by means of ideas. Too many plays seek to recreate events; this one presages an event. It is to a revolution what an architect's sketch is to a completed building. This attempt is based on the aesthetic principle that reality in and of itself is boring, because it represents only content. Only its transcendence by means of imagination — in other words, its use by an idea — gives the material transparency and fire. (G, 20)

The turning to the present — and by implication to the future — which had already been indicated in the frame of *Soldiers,* was to be completed in *Guerillas.* Yet the aesthetic position which Hochhuth described in the introduction was not so different from that which he had held in 1963 and throughout the intervening years. It was still a political theater that considered itself as a "moralische Anstalt," and Hochhuth still advocated a classical dramatic form which would provide a transcendence from the everyday world of politics to the realm of ideas, providing a model for the future. The legitimate link between Hochhuth's drama and the drama of Schiller which thus still existed is best illustrated by the fact that in the *Vorwort* Hochhuth used a quotation from Schiller to support his concept of Realism. "'The modern [writer] struggles laboriously and fearfully with accidental and secondary matters, and he loads himself down with empty and insignificant things in an attempt to come close to reality; and by doing that he runs the risk of losing the profound truth which inheres in everything poetic. He would like to completely imitate an actual occurrence and does not reflect that a poetic representation can never coincide with reality, because it [the poetic] is absolutely true'" (G, 21).[6]

There are some interesting similarities between the view of political drama Hochhuth broaches in this introduction and those presented by Peter Weiss in his 1968 essay, "Das Material und die Modelle: Notizen zum dokumentarischen Drama." Despite Hochhuth's continued rejection of the term "documentary drama" and Weiss' acceptance of it, both authors stress the poetic nature of the theater, agreeing that it has a truth of its own which cannot duplicate the newscast or the documentary film. For both dramatists, political theater involved something more than the mere reconstruction of events; both emphasized the selection and arrangement of the material by the author. But the differences that a closer examination of their statements reveals can help us to better understand Hochhuth's unique position in the West German drama of the 1960s and 1970s.

Whereas for Hochhuth the work of art itself presents the audience with a kind of absolute truth, while ideology could only give a partial one, for Weiss just the opposite was true. Hochhuth rejected all ideology and retained a "third position" in the East-West conflict, while Weiss had struggled to liberate himself from a bourgeois upbringing and had finally abandoned his "third position" in favor of Marxism.[7] After that change Weiss could accept the fact that the work of art might distort reality if it could stand for the absolute truth he had found in ideology. By the time Weiss wrote "Das Material und die Modelle" he had entirely shed that absurd view of life which had colored his early plays in favor of a position which maintained that "das dokumentarische Theater ist parteilich."[8] It is understandable why Hochhuth had such a negative attitude toward a term that was defined by his contemporary as a partisan theater. Weiss believed in a political drama which would take sides in the ideological struggle of a divided world, but he did not believe that documentary drama could recreate an event. Like Hochhuth he felt that the drama worked on the principle of concentration.[9] Like Hochhuth he also pointed to the essential difference between drama and the "happening" or street demonstration, between drama and the newscast.[10] But he also placed greater emphasis on *Berichterstattung* (reporting) and less on the poetic imagination, on the transcendence to the realm of ideas.[11]

The most important difference between the two writers is revealed when Weiss gives examples of how documentary material might be utilized in a drama: "Individual conflicts are not portrayed, but socially or economically dictated patterns of behavior are. The documentary theater, in contrast to the other media, which are quickly consumed, is concerned with the exemplary, it does not work with dramatis personae and sketches of milieu, but with groups, forces, tendencies."[12] Hochhuth was also concerned with the exemplary, but he still believed in the "personalization of conflicts." Thus where Hochhuth wished to preserve a dramatic form with individual characters, Weiss advocated the dissolution of the techniques of traditional drama and called for a revolutionary art that would overturn conventional aesthetic categories. Although the shift from past to future represented a significant change in Hochhuth's dramatic theory and practice, it was hardly "revolutionary." The techniques which he used in *Guerillas* did not markedly differ from those used in his first two plays. Once again, the conflict of ideas was to be presented by using individual characters as the carriers of those ideas.

## II   Guerillas: *A Tragedy*

The idea that obsessed Hochhuth in his third tragedy was the strategy of revolutionary change which he had already elaborated in his political essays. In the introduction to the play he explained at length why he had selected the United States rather than West Germany as the setting for his revolution. No doubt he wanted to ward off the repeated criticism that he was always attacking other countries than his own. The United States had been chosen, however, because it was at the center of the capitalist system while West Germany was but a satellite. And the revolution had to begin at the center, where the soil was fertile and politically volcanic: "No one fells a tree by breaking off a limb" (G, 17). Furthermore, the USA appeared to be an exaggeration of Western European conditions, and "exaggeration clarifies" (G, 17).

Thus Hochhuth actually intended to write a play about the United States only in order to give an example to Western Europeans. This may explain, in part, why the play has been virtually ignored in the country which is the locus of the dramatic action; it was never intended for an American audience. As one German critic so aptly put it: "His analysis is superb and may even have an enlightening effect in this country; the synthesis leaves something to be desired. It is, after all, a play by a German written for Germans. America's left can get along without Hochhuth: 'You don't need a weatherman to know which way the wind blows' (Bob Dylan)."[13]

Hochhuth needed to make a few revisions in his dramatic form to accommodate the new methodology as well as to demonstrate a specific political strategy. The major change was that he could no longer draw on prominent figures of the recent past for his protagonist or antagonist but had to create fictional personages to carry the conflict of ideas into the imaginary, yet imaginable future. But actually there was little difference between the entirely fictional figures of *Guerillas* and the mixed dramatis personae — some historical, some fictional — of the two previous plays. The individualized characters were still treated realistically, and the author continued to caution that they were not Naturalistic: "So wenig wie ihre Sprache sind die Menschen, die hier agieren, naturalistisch abgehorcht und gesehen — sie sind Ideenträger" (G, 20).

Hochhuth's guerillas are, in fact, the small elite of "decent" men about whom he had spoken in the political essays. Many of them are members of the ruling oligarchy they plan to overthrow, and at their head is a United States senator, David L. Nicolson, young, handsome, intelligent, and wealthy.[14] Ironically, the profits from his companies are being channeled into activities that will attempt to destroy the very system which has accounted for his personal fortune. Dialogue is still the primary means for carrying forward a plot that begins with the meeting between Senator Nicolson and one of his guerillas on Park Avenue in New York and ends with the death of the chief conspirator. The words of the first scene are thus echoed in the last, for in discussing a plan to kidnap and kill a judge, Nicolson suggests it should be done in such a way that suicide cannot be ruled out (G, 28). Similarly, when the CIA agent makes Nicolson jump out of the window to his death in the final scene (Act V, Scene 2), it is done in such a way that suicide will be assumed.

Being an entirely fictional character, Nicolson is better able to fit the mold of tragic hero than either of the protagonists of the two previous dramas. Yet the turn to an imagined future also entailed a disadvantage. The figure of the senator lacks the immediate interest that Pope Pius XII or Churchill — even a Riccardo, who was based on specific historical models — could inspire. In the essay "Über Zeitereignis und Dichtung" ("Contemporary History and Litera-ture"), Max Frisch, the Swiss dramatist, had argued that a play which chooses recent history or current events as its subject matter has "an advance effect" which is illegitimate, since the dramaturgy is ignored in favor of the content. And the involvement of the audience is assured, since everyone is an expert on the subject.[15] Whether legitimate or not, Hochhuth's first two plays certainly benefited from this "Vorschuß an Wirkung," ("advance effect"). And no matter how much current interest there might be in revolu-tionary tactics, Guerillas could not hope to elicit the same response, because Nicolson was not a contemporary figure and lacked the depth of character of a Pius XII or a Churchill. All too easily he be-came the mouthpiece for Hochhuth's theory of infiltration. This time, it seemed, critical appraisal would have to be based more on the drama's literary merit.

One of the advantages of working with a fictional protagonist, however, was that the author could more readily provide his character with a tragic flaw. Nicolson's flaw is the traditional hubris. As one of the conspirators foresees in the first scene of the play, the leader does not follow his own best advice (G, 27). Instead of restricting his activities to the Northern hemisphere, he is simultaneously involved in guerilla warfare in Latin America, evidently linked to Che Guevara's movement in Bolivia. Although this secondary interest seems natural, since his wife is Argentinian, Nicolson overextends himself and must appoint her as a messenger. This proves his undoing, for Maria, who is described as completely apolitical (G, 41), after unwittingly tipping off the CIA about her husband's South American liaisons, is captured, raped, and killed in Guatemala. But Stryker, the CIA agent who discovers the plot, is also the senator's personal friend. In order to save face he forces Nicolson to jump out of the window, rather than suffer exposure, thus ironically preventing the discovery of the major conspiracy.

Yet Stryker, who by rights should be the antagonist in the conflict of ideas, is not given the intellectual stature to assume this role, his sentiments being narrow-minded and blindly patriotic. Hochhuth tried to solve the problem by distributing the antagonistic role in the realm of ideas among several other characters, but he only succeeded in diluting the arguments that countered those of Nicolson. This lack of a central antagonist, identical in the action and in the conflict of ideas, constitutes one of the major weaknesses of the play. Both Maria Nicolson and Professor Wiener, a family friend and business associate, question the need for violence. But the beautiful wife is too wrapped up in her own personal dilemma — her inability to bear children — to be an effective antagonist. In addition, as a woman she is seen primarily as a sex object by the characters and the author alike (G, 41).[16] Her opposition never goes beyond the emotional level, and eventually she blindly follows her husband's lead.

At least briefly in Act IV, Professor Wiener and Nicolson engage in a conversation that pits the opposing views on the important question of force against each other. Wiener advocates the creation of a new opposition party. He seems to echo Hochhuth's earlier views when he states: "The conservative is, accordingly, *more humane,* because he is satisfied with changing *institutions* because of his insight into the eternally unchanging nature of man — instead of wanting to improve man himself, which can only happen with the help of terror" (G, 157).[17] But Nicolson abruptly retorts: "Institutions also can only be changed by means of terror" (G, 157). Instead of using his wealth and influence to create a viable worker's party, as Wiener suggests, he assures his guerillas access to an atomic submarine, which his own shipping company is building, so that they can threaten the government at the time of the coup. Like Hochhuth in the essay "Angst vor der 'Schutz'-Macht USA," Nicolson tends to think in absolutes. He insists that infiltration and coup d'état are the only means for revolution in the United States because they are ultimately the only way to avoid anarchy: "Therefore like Mirabeau I want to prevent a bloodbath by means of the coup d'état, which is the only legal way to bring about social revolution. Every violent act that is provoked by the oppressors is legal" (G, 155). Thus the tragic hero, for whom the dramatist tries to arouse our sympathy, moves dangerously close to a position which Hochhuth had so eloquently argued against in *Soldiers* — that any end justifies the means.

Hochhuth's use of realistic time and place in *Guerillas* is also similar to the corresponding features in his first two plays. He divided the tragedy into the traditional five acts. The first act is subdivided into three scenes which introduce Nicolson's two spheres of involvement. By moving from New York to Bolivia (Act I, Scene 3), they provide a detailed exposition and suggest the reason for the hero's ultimate end. Act II continues in the South American setting, but changes from a specific location in a hacienda onto a moon-flooded plain. Hochhuth specifically asks that there be no props in this scene (G, 99), thus suggesting a timelessness similar to that which he had tried to achieve in the framework of *Soldiers*. At this juncture, he also briefly abandons the dialogue form and allows the protagonist to turn directly to the audience in a poetic monologue. The language of the passage is elevated, and the dramatist emphasizes this aspect by having Nicolson speak this "obituary for freedom" in an "entirely anti-Naturalistic fashion, in the old monologue form, up front, stage center" (G, 109–10).[18]

Act III then returns us to the active world of the conspirators, this time in New London, Connecticut, where a group of them eliminate a diver who is nosing around the Nicolson shipyard. Act IV takes place on Nicolson's mother's yacht and is an occasion for further subterfuge, since both Nicolson and Stryker are present; but, more important for the conflict of ideas, it allows Wiener and Nicolson to exchange views on the revolution. In the final act, our attention is again briefly directed to the Latin American scene, when Maria is captured in a Guatemalan church, an event that constitutes the dramatic climax. The last scene, in Nicolson's New

York law office, precipitates the catastrophe, once Stryker has broken the painful news of Maria's death. But although the plot thus proceeds linearly, with a loosely causal relationship between the realistic scenes, it often abandons verisimilitude. This cops and robbers aspect of the play may be due, in part, to Hochhuth's turning away from historical material to an entirely fictional reality. But although the author states specifically that *Guerillas* is neither an historical nor a documentary drama, he does not entirely abandon his use of documentary material in his third tragedy.

Throughout the drama he subtly undermines the apparently imaginary plot with its fictional characters by choosing a readily definable historical era as the background for the action, which falls quite clearly into the period immediately preceding the 1968 presidential election. Specific references are made to the upcoming Democratic convention in Chicago, for which student demonstrations are being planned in conjunction with Nicolson's conspiracy (G, 71). Hochhuth also includes long prose passages, similar to those found in *The Deputy* and *Soldiers,* to create a specific historical setting. Each scene is also preceded by a quotation from a newspaper article, book or, in one case, from Che Guevara's diary, which help the reader to decipher specific references subsequently made in the dialogue. In fact, very little is left to the imagination of the reader or even the theater audience, since, in addition to these expository sections, the dialogue also contains countless references to figures from current affairs: the Kennedy family, Richard Nixon, President Johnson, Che Guevara, Cardinal Spellman, and Jimmy Hoffa, to name only a few. But Hochhuth went beyond the blending in of historical references and the use of supplementary documentary material to make innuendoes, which, although not a major factor in the plot, are nevertheless reminiscent of his treatment of the Churchill-Sikorski affair in *Soldiers.* He suggests, for example, that the FBI knew of John Kennedy's assassination and was even planning that of Robert Kennedy. And in a rather offhand manner he suggests some connection between Richard Nixon and the tragic events in Dallas (G, 125).

But Hochhuth in this play seemed to have greater difficulty in integrating his particular political or historical thesis, buttressed by documentary evidence, with the tragic action. Perhaps this was so because the dramatist wanted to use the drama itself in order to expound his theory of infiltration, even though he had already done so in the political essays that had prepared the way; he therefore chose a new device to lengthen the drama without introducing a subplot, as he had in *Soldiers*. Between each of the eight major scenes outlined above he inserted brief scenes entitled *Vorbühne* (to be played in front of the curtain). Despite his supposed rejection of *Verfremdung,* he relied here on the Brechtian device of banners (*Schriften*) to identify the locale of each scene, since no elaborate stage sets were called for. Six of the eight scenes could be considered as peripheral to the main plot; they feature a variety of conspirators in a number of different locations, thus highlighting the nature of the conspiracy and the scope of its operation. The last, for example, takes place in the computer center of the Pentagon and shows the extent to which the infiltration strategy had succeeded in penetrating the oligarchy (G, 186–90). On the whole the scenes are devoted more to discussion than to action.

Two of the scenes do not follow this pattern but are reminiscent of the satirical sketches that Hochhuth included in the framework of *Soldiers*. Each of them has a cabaretlike quality; they could be performed entirely separately from the play and still be understood. The first, *Vorbühne* II, takes place in a jail (G, 48–54). The two figures are treated anonymously, but the scene is nevertheless very specific, for the rich visitor is trying to get the unnamed prisoner to help in the plan to assassinate Martin Luther King. The scene's only apparent function is to further authenticate the specific historical setting of the play. The second scene of this type, *Vorbühne* V, seems entirely extraneous. It is entitled "The President's Limousine" (G, 114–17). Although Nicolson appears briefly, in order to contact one of his guerillas, it adds nothing to the plot or to the understanding of the conspiracy. Canning, a journalist and one of the conspirators, is doing a story on the President's new armored car. His questions and the replies of the official who is demonstrating the automobile simply provide a comical interlude, an ironic commentary on "the land of the free and the home of the brave" which interrupts the dramatic action. Even a few of the characters in the major scenes indicate Hochhuth's growing interest in comedy and political satire. Bobby, Stryker's constant companion, is a parody of the musclebound, brainless body guard. Nicolson's Mom, also a comic figure, turns out to be one of the most effective, as the epitome of high society, a Daughter of the American Revolution and woman's club president, whose concern for the poor is genuine but somewhat misplaced.

Despite Hochhuth's new political militance, as revealed in the essays written before and after the publication of *Guerillas,* the drama itself lacked any formal features which could be considered radical departures from his previous practice. He continued to write a traditional tragedy of ideas, only now using entirely fictional characters. But the demise of the hero still takes place in a relatively realistic setting supported by documentary material. Even the occasional use of a satirical sketch was not entirely new, because Hochhuth had experimented with a similar technique in the framework of *Soldiers.* Although the use of the short *Vorbühne* scenes might be considered a legitimate innovation, most of them were but a tiresome expansion of his political theory. Significantly, when the play was first produced, these scenes were eliminated in order to reduce the playing time to a more reasonable three hours.[19] The lack of radical changes in dramatic form can be accounted for, I think, by the fact that Hochhuth's *Weltanschauung* — of which his dramas are always a reflection — had remained unchanged. World view and dramatic form continued to complement one another as one German critic, Hellmuth Karasek, had to admit grudgingly: "That Hochhuth considers it possible to present his world view in the five acts of a tragedy has to do with his conviction that history depends upon the men who make it. Adorno's controversy with Hochhuth apropos of *The Deputy* could be rekindled again here."[20]

But neither the political arguments raised in this *Bühnenpamphlet* (stage pamphlet) nor its use of a traditional dramaturgy could really rekindle the flames of controversy to the intense white heat that had characterized the aftermath of the first two plays. As usual, however, Hochhuth's play did arouse some controversy as soon as it was published and performed in Germany. He was called a conservative by some, while others openly used the word "fascist."[21] Hochhuth once again found himself on the defensive, especially politically, as is evidenced by his concentration on the infiltration strategy in "Keine Revolution ohne Infiltration." But the strategy of coup d'état was hardly new or radical either. The play just did not have the same *Zündkraft* (explosiveness) as its predecessors. More importantly, as Karasek suggested, *Guerillas* added nothing to the aesthetic controversy that Hochhuth had first aroused with *The Deputy,* and it is for that reason, too, that the reactions remained muted. Although the play experienced fifteen different productions, it never penetrated beyond the borders of Germany, Austria and Switzerland.

The first production, in May 1970, under the direction of Peter Palitzsch, at the Württembergisches Staatstheater received mixed reviews; the director was praised for having left out the unnecessary *Vorbühne* scenes, thus narrowing the focus of the drama to its *Kernthese* (core thesis) which was repeated like a leitmotif from beginning to end: "For two hundred million [people]! Against two hundred millionaires!"[22] Once again the inevitable comparisons with Schillerian drama were made. But Karasek noted that the term *Pyrrhusniederlage* (pyrrhic defeat) — if there was such a thing — most nearly described Hochhuth's success story, for every time he wrote a play, it was first greeted with a "'So-kann-man-doch-kein-Drama-schreiben'-Geschrei" ("You-can't-write-drama-that-way-cry"), then performed and debated around the world; but this description more nearly fits the reactions to *The Deputy* and *Soldiers* than *Guerillas.* The third tragedy simply failed to elicit a worldwide response. Perhaps the necessary "advance effect" was missing this time, despite the topical theme. And without it, Hochhuth's dramaturgy could not stand on its own. Left without history as a source for his major characters, Hochhuth was not able to breathe the same life into his fictional creations. The satirical ones, like "Mom," seemed more vibrant, more "realistic" in Hochhuth's sense, than the hero Nicolson or his antagonist Stryker. But too much of the drama was taken up with seemingly fruitless strategy discussions among the conspirators. Much of the time was spent creating alibis for their meeting in the first place. Certain scenes, especially in Act III when the frogman is killed in the shipyard, come across simply as "kintoppmäßig albern" ("silly, like in the movies").[23] Perhaps, as at least one critic argued, Hochhuth's impassioned pleas for a redistribution of wealth, for a social revolution, could not be overheard, but the form of the play seems to detract from, rather than enhance, the argument. The audience is more likely to identify with the confused Maria or the conservative Professor Wiener than with the radical hero.

It is significant that not only Hochhuth himself, in his defense of the play, but also many of his critics, concentrating on his political views, overlooked the fact that by writing a tragedy, Hochhuth had not provided a model for the future revolution after all. Instead of a utopia, we encounter a coup that apparently fails. The revolutionaries are reduced to discussion, to two bumbling attempts to do away with petty spies, and to reliance on an apolitical female who gives it all away; and the play ends with the supposed suicide of their leader, leaving the success of the coup in doubt. It was only by means of a change in orientation — the move from tragedy to comedy — that Hochhuth was able, in his next two plays, *Die Hebamme* and *Lysistrate und die Nato,* to provide more positive revolutionary models. And, ironically, in both cases women become the successful protagonists in the revolt against poverty and war.

## CHAPTER 6

# The Comedies

## I  A Tragic View of Life

**H**OCHHUTH continued in the period after 1970 to punctuate his dramatic works with essayistic endeavors. But those immediately following *Guerillas* seemed to add little new to either his political or his aesthetic theories. He dealt with specific issues, speaking out strongly against the Vietnam War at the Frankfurt demonstrations in May 1970, for instance. His appeal to the defense minister, "Appell an Verteidigungsminister Schmidt," was included a year later in the volume *Die Hebamme (The Midwife),* which contained poems, essays, and prose works as well as Hochhuth's first comedy (H, 327–34). Another topic which interested Hochhuth at that point was the fate of the struggling writer in West German society. This was the subject of another appeal, "Unsere 'abgeschriebenen' Schriftsteller in der Bundesrepublik" ("Our writers in the Federal Republic who are 'written off,'" [ H, 335–46]). More importantly, he issued a plea to Chancellor Willy Brandt in behalf of slum dwellers, the central topic of his comedy (K, 247–49). This open letter was dated March 6, 1971, and had been published in *Krieg und Klassenkrieg* in August 1971, three months before the appearance of *Die Hebamme.* But the choice of this subject was not surprising, since Hochhuth had already demonstrated his concern in the 1965 essay "Der Klassenkampf ist nicht zu Ende" (K, 23–24). Only now he not only pointed to the fact that nearly one million West Germans live in slum housing in the midst of the "economic miracle," but also suggested his own particular solution to the problem: Landlords with available housing must be forced by law to rent to former slum residents, and the government must subsidize this effort by paying the difference between the actual rent and what the new tenants could afford. Above all Hochhuth rejected the idea of subsidized housing projects, which, in his opinion, would simply create new ghettos. He insisted on the need to disperse the residents throughout any given city (K, 249). His suggestion must stand on its own merits, but it is interesting to note Hochhuth's legislative approach, which stands in direct contrast to that suggested in *Die Hebamme*. What is characteristic in both the essay and the comedy, however, is the sense of urgency with which his proposals are made, because as Hochhuth puts it, "all the measures that have been used up to this point in the Federal Republic, as the statistics show, have not brought us *one step further* toward the elimination of the slums" (K, 249).

In addition to such issue-oriented statements, Hochhuth wrote a lengthy treatise on history during this period between plays. "Der alte Mythos vom 'neuen' Menschen: Vorstudie zu einer Ethologie der Geschichte" ("The old myth of the 'new' man: preliminary study to an ethology of history") was published in part in *konkret* in 1969 and lengthened for inclusion in the *Hebamme* collection (H, 374). In it Hochhuth elaborated all his previously stated political views, but, more significantly for us, gave some insight into the reason for the change from tragedy to comedy.

Earlier, in discussion with students, Hochhuth had suggested that part of the misunderstanding between them might be due to the fact that they read the wrong Marcuse, Herbert instead of Ludwig.[1] The treatise expanded on this insight, directly refuting the former's concept of the "new" man and espousing the so-called "pessimism" of the latter.[2] In addition to the thought of Ludwig Marcuse and Oswald Spengler, Hochhuth relied here again on the ideas of the philosopher Karl Jaspers, and on still another professor of the University of Basle — albeit during the nineteenth century — Jakob Burckhardt, whom he calls a humanist skeptic (H, 359) — a term one might well apply to Hochhuth himself.

Although Hochhuth feels that there are things in society that must be radically changed, he cannot support the view of Herbert Marcuse that one must first change the very nature of man. Change (*Veränderung*) is possible, but improvement (*Verbesserung*) is not (H, 380). For the study of human behavior in history (ethology) teaches us that man's basic nature is stable. Man is not on the way to some final utopia; he does not really progress, for history continues to move in cyclical patterns. Hochhuth points to the rise and fall of civilizations. "Every history book refutes the optimism of a final goal" (H, 399). Since man cannot be basically improved, each generation must criticize, or even overturn, the institutions that have been handed down to it. Hochhuth thus appears to advocate a kind of perpetual revolution.[3] His formula for history is "von vorne beginnen" ("begin from the beginning," or "begin all over again"). He calls this "Sisyphus-Arbeit" ("the work of Sisyphus") (H, 369). But the fact that there is no real progress from one generation to the next does not suggest passivity, for the final meaning of life lies in the absurd activity itself. "There is no purpose beyond the life of a generation; we do not go upward but onward" (H, 370).

According to Hochhuth, the great moral enemy is not to be found in man himself, but in the realities of power politics. Excessive concentrations of power, like those of the dangerous "Goliaths," the USSR and the USA, must be resisted. But how should one go about this? Hochhuth answers in this essay, as he had before, that it is the individual — that is, the few outstanding individuals in every age — who carry the weight of historical change: "It is always a matter of the individual, whether he or she conforms within an organization or whether he or she remains a personality; that means, the organization *conforms*" (H, 363–64). Character, and not ideology, is thus important — not what a man believes but who he is. Hochhuth once again launches an attack against all religions or political ideologies that claim to have a complete answer. He repeats his warning against the dogmatism of Marxist ideology in particular. "The Marxists have only interpreted Marx differently, but it is necessary to change him" (H, 375). Marxists must be willing to revise Marx, and all men must learn to do without a closed view of the world ("geschlossenes Weltbild"; "heiles Weltbild"). For Hochhuth, the discovery of a utopia diverts man from the real problems of the world. "Whereas in only thirty years nothing will be more interesting for seven billion inhabitants of the globe than the question, Where do we get bread — this last philosopher of the decadent bourgeoisie [Herbert Marcuse] projects his secularized heaven, which has as much to do with this world as the heaven of Dante, onto the screen in dust-free, fully climate-controlled lecture rooms to the sons of such fathers as have the money to let their offspring study." (H, 391).

Although Herbert Marcuse must take the brunt of Hochhuth's

criticism in this essay, as Adorno had to do earlier, the dramatist might just as well have attacked his fellow writer, Peter Weiss, who had consciously searched for a world view as complete as that of Dante and found it in Marxism.[4] For Hochhuth, however, neither Dante's vision of the world with its heaven, nor Herbert Marcuse's vision of a future Garden of Eden in which even the animals will have abandoned their natural aggressiveness, have any relevance to the world we live in. Instead, like the Existentialist, Albert Camus, he chooses Sisyphus as the figure who best expresses the unalterable condition of mankind, and, at the same time, man's unceasing struggle to work toward change.[5] Sisyphus represents the quintessence of Hochhuth's conception of the politically engaged man. In the letter to the Czech writer Mňačko Hochhuth had already drawn attention to this parallel, calling the task of man "the struggle for the realization of the idea of freedom, its great tragic Sisyphus game [play]" (K, 95). In the essay "Der alte Mythos vom 'neuen' Menschen" he explores the analogy even further:

I am not a defeatist. To repeat: the more pressing the awareness of our fate, the more vehemently can it fire up the activity in us to help avert this constraint [*Zwang*]. Sisyphus is not a mythical figure, but the politically most exemplary; even the "crime" which led to his punishment makes him eternally sympathetic and present; the reviling of the "master"! Politics always begins with the rebellion against an authority; the dignity of man begins when he says to a "master" that he does not recognize him. (H, 400)

Hochhuth, like Camus, interprets the figure of Sisyphus in a positive way, laying special emphasis on the dignity that he achieves as an individual. Although Hochhuth is not blindly optimistic about man's ability to change, he considers it an absolute necessity for him to try to alter his present environment in concrete ways. He therefore allows in this basically tragic view of life for a certain amount of forward motion, even if it cannot be called "progress" toward a final goal, but simply eternal repetition. Despite the tragic overtones, Sisyphus does suggest an absurd figure, and it is perhaps because of this realization that Hochhuth made the shift from tragedy to comedy at this juncture. It was, however, a change in emphasis rather than substance, for it simply brought into the foreground his long-held belief that our existence, when considered most realistically, is in fact full of absurdity. Thus a tragic view of life, with never-changing man at its center, provides the background for his comedies. What Hochhuth wished to illustrate in them was the *Sisyphus-Arbeit* itself. These are goals that can be reached through the efforts of individuals within a single generation (H, 415). "Sisyphus will eternally symbolize the struggle of man with history. Between mankind and the gate to a paradise, like the one Herbert Marcuse envisions, lies and remains lying, the rock of Sisyphus. The necessity of moving it gives the motor of the world comedy its never-ending propellant" (H, 420–21).

Hochhuth's use of the word *Weltkomödie* here is significant. It is reminiscent of his use of the idea of a "kleines Welttheater" in *Soldiers.* But the emphasis has shifted from the tragic to the comic aspect of the world as stage, for Hochhuth now felt he could better demonstrate the work that had to be done in this way. In the two comedies which were to follow each other in quick succession, *Die Hebamme* (1971) and *Lysistrate und die Nato* (1973), Hochhuth dealt in turn with the two most difficult problems he had referred to in the essay — poverty and war. In each comedy, a heroine manages to bring about a certain amount of change. And yet the "progress" that is made is Sisyphean. Through comic actions that are even pushed to the point of the absurd, a "happy ending" is achieved, while the ultimately tragic backdrop of the world stage remains. Yet both heroines are characterized as real individuals who exercise their free will within a given social and political milieu. Significantly, both women are active in local and/or national politics; both are elected officials, and yet they seek nonparliamentary ways of changing the status quo. Both try to change their reality, like Sisyphus, in the most elementary kind of rebellion, the rejection of authority. But in both cases, the "happy ending" is overshadowed by the awareness of the larger context in which their final victories have been achieved.

## II  Die Hebamme: *Justice versus Law*

Hochhuth had been promising for a long time to write this comedy; he even referred to it by the name of "Die Gemeindeschwester" ("The Community Nurse") as early as October 1967.[6] In addition to such specific references, there were numerous other indications in the late 1960s that Hochhuth felt increasingly drawn to the comic mode. The parodistic characters in *Guerillas* are one such herald; another is his "rhymed commentaries" on political subjects entitled "Deutschland braucht Bayern" ("Germany needs Bavaria," [H, 303–14]), and also the satirical playlet, "Zigarillos," published in *Die Zeit* in September 1970.[7] But as the author later stated in an interview, the comic element had always been his concern: "One cannot be continually preoccupied with the history of Hitler's Germany, for example, without going crazy. In addition, from the beginning I have always conceived of humorous topics at the same time as the serious ones. It was really a matter of chance that I first brought the serious material to the public. Most of all I would like to write only comedies — there is no lack of material."[8]

But Hochhuth in the same interview also admitted that his turn to comedy did not really reflect a different intent. The theater was still to be used as a forum for presenting a conflict of ideas in order to bring a pressing moral or political issue to the attention of the public. In fact, the comical treatment of character, the use of farce, and the "happy ending" barely conceal the utter seriousness of the topic chosen for discussion in *Die Hebamme*. A quotation from Stendhal opening the epilogue typifies what actually happened to Hochhuth when he was writing this comedy. "'And that is the unlucky star of our times: the author wanted to devote himself to humorous things, but his scenes were darkened in the end by the political misery'" (H, 287).[9]

Hochhuth's dramaturgy remained virtually intact despite the shift to comedy. *Die Hebamme* continued the pattern already well established by *Guerillas* of using entirely fictional dramatis personae in a realistic setting, buttressed by the use of documentary material. Once again each scene was preceded by quotations from newspaper reports that drew parallels to the action. Descriptive passages, although somewhat shorter than in the previous plays, again presented the political and economic views of the author and his analyses of the characters.

All the characters in *Die Hebamme* are treated as real individuals, although there are no figures of historical importance among them; nor do they represent an imaginary elite, but rather — as was traditionally the case in comedy — the "little man." The heroine, Sophie, is the best described as an individual, whereas the others are comically stereotyped, a fact that is underscored by the assigning of names like Rosentreter (treads on roses) to the Catholic priest, alluding to the *Rosenkranz* (rosary); Neuweiher (new initiator) to the chief obstetrician, alluding to his role of bringing newborns into the world; or Senkblei (sinking lead) to the representative of the military. This too is simply an old comedy technique used to advantage. Even the heroine's name suggests the unconventional "wisdom" which she preaches and practices.

The action of *Die Hebamme,* although set in the Adenauer era, is based on an incident that occurred in Kassel in the summer of 1971 and to which direct reference is made in the dialogue. A group of poor people moved into some abandoned *Bundeswehr* (West German army) barracks and were forcibly removed by the police, even though they had received verbal guarantees from the local authorities that they would not be evicted. In the play the heroine, an old midwife, reveals that she has been masquerading for fifteen years as the widow of a field marshal, Frau von Hossenbach, a personal friend whom she had buried herself and whose personal papers she had kept while destroying her own. With the substantial pension she thus receives illegally, Sophie helps the poor who are her special charge as a CDU member of the city council of Wilhelmsthal, an imaginary town in Hesse. But she becomes even further embroiled in illegal activities when she encourages the residents of a slum, "Chicago-North," to burn down their dwellings and move into a new development for army bandmasters. Sophie also carries out her plan to provide permanent care for the elderly of the slum in a new nursing home run by Rosentreter. Ironically, in her role as Frau von Hossenbach she gets the army musicians to move the old people, while in her role as Sophie she simultaneously prepares the occupation of their houses. In addition, as Sophie she takes money that had been collected to build a Lutheran church and parsonage, in order, as Frau von Hossenbach, to give it to Rosentreter for his worthier cause. Much of the comic effect of the play is achieved by this traditional technique of double identity, which reaches a climax in the final scene (*Bild* 8), when the director of the military band academy is laughed out of the courtroom for mistaking Sophie for the baroness, while Rosentreter, who knows the truth, skillfully avoids telling it. The audience can laugh at all those who — unlike them — don't know the full story.

In this final scene Hochhuth also relies on the traditional comedy situation of the courtroom. Landgerichtsdirektor Bläbberberg seems to know even less than Dorfrichter Adam in Heinrich von

Kleist's *Der zerbrochene Krug (The Broken Jug)* how to keep order in a courtroom, but unlike Adam he is successful in covering up his part in the "crime."[10] Ironically, Sophie is brought to trial at her own insistence, for she hopes in this way to get a legal guarantee that the poor people can remain in the occupied housing. She does this not so much by means of eloquent speeches as by her refusal to reveal why she has turned over the Lutheran minister's funds to Frau von Hossenbach. She thinks that her silence will force the local politicians to concede, but unbeknownst to her, entirely different motivations bring about the eventual happy resolution. The audience, however, is allowed to watch the machinations of the city fathers, Bläbberberg (CDU), Gnilljeneimer (SPD), and Koggelgritz (FDP), representing the three major West German political parties. They do not arrive at any true realization of the needs of the poor; what is important to them is the "image" of the town, and they cleverly use the situation to serve their own personal ends, in some cases receiving direct payoffs in the form of land or money. Thus even the apparent "happy end" has an ironic twist, for as Sophie-Sisyphus dies in the courtroom, satisfied that she has brought her rock to the top of the hill, we in the audience are aware that, left to these representatives of law and order, it will soon roll down once more.

Even the victims in Hochhuth's play are not spared the harsh light of satire. Sophie barely succeeds in convincing them of the need to burn their homes. Many are reluctant to follow her lead. And she says at one point, in utter frustration, "Must I think of everything, you're men after all" (H, 214).[11] But although the entire thrust of the plot and the characterization, with its use of dialect humor, is comic, Sophie is taken quite seriously by the author. She incorporates for him the kind of Sisyphean effort of which he had spoken in the essay "Der alte Mythos vom 'neuen' Menschen." In his view, her revolt against authority constitutes a genuinely revolutionary act. There can be no doubt that despite the use of comedy as a medium, Hochhuth wanted to appeal directly to the moral sense of his audience on the issue of poverty and slum housing. In a discussion with Rosentreter in *Bild* 5, Sophie reveals not only the extent of her civil disobedience, but the reasons for her revolt. And Rosentreter is forced to admit: "Whoever abides by the law, goes against morality" (H, 188). Sophie distinguishes between *Recht* (justice) on the one hand, and *Gesetz* (law) on the other. Unlike nearly all the other characters in the play except Rosentreter himself, she never takes money for her own profit; Hossenbach's pension goes entirely to the poor. As she explains to the priest: "No one shall ever be able to accuse me of having violated *justice,* only because I myself made a *law,* which out of hard-heartedness those who are responsible for doing it in parliament have neglected to pass" (H, 186). In defending her actions before the court Sophie makes a similar distinction: "Knowingly I have never acted unjustly. However a life under German lawmakers has taught me that whoever wants to help a just cause find justice in this land must often break laws" (H, 258). The emphasis here is on breaking laws, rather than making new ones, as in Hochhuth's letter to Chancellor Brandt, but such a statement clearly reflects the author's increasingly militant position since 1968. He had stated that as an engaged author he must remain true to his own conception of moral rectitude, just like Sophie, even if it led him to make statements that were "dangerous to youth, treasonous, even asocial to the point of being criminal" (K, 97–98). Some critics would maintain that both *Guerillas* and *Die Hebamme* contain such statements because of the apparent advocacy of civil disobedience — even violence — to bring about change. But, interestingly, the comedy aroused more controversy in Germany than the tragedy.

The critical reception of *Die Hebamme* was for the most part negative. Hellmuth Karasek, for example, accused Hochhuth of having fascist tendencies, on the grounds that his central tenet, which places individual initiative above authority, is a step in the direction of the "call for a strong man." Karasek also objected to Hochhuth's style. He attempted his own brand of humor in characterizing what he considered to be the author's humorlessness. "Hochhuth has an intimate relationship to humor which resembles that of a seal to the Sahara." He objected in particular to the dialect humor and to the stereotyping of characters, even though these are well-known comedy techniques, saying of the play as a whole that it "has the depth of a beer puddle on a *Stammtisch* [table reserved for regular customers]."[12] The *Dramaturg* of the Kassel theater, which had decided to produce the play, rushed to Hochhuth's defense. Once again Hochhuth was in the center of controversy: "I consider an apparent comedy conclusion like this one, where everything works out the way it never would be resolved in reality, to be more provocative, more conducive to reflection, than the explicit call for a change of the situation (which, in addition, doesn't change unless many people develop 'individual' initiative and responsibility; this appears clear to me and is not at all fascist)."[13] But both the critic and the apologist ignored the fact that the "solution" offered by the play is not even very satisfactory in that context.

One might also ask whether comedy is the proper medium for treating the question of the justification of illegal acts by individuals. Whether the seriousness of purpose behind the comedy will be recognized by the audience will depend almost entirely on the treatment the text receives at the hands of a director. This was clearly indicated by the reviews of first performances, held nearly simultaneously in Kassel, Munich, and Zurich. The most successful production in this respect was the one in Kassel, where the topic was particularly appropriate. Kai Braak, the director, chose a Piscator technique; by juxtaposing the scenes of the comedy with a documentary film on the slums of Kassel he was able to make the audience both reflect on and be amused by the issue. Peter Iden remarked in his critique: "From this contrast between the authenticity of the film and the repeatedly interrupted fiction of the satire the evening gained tension [and] achieved its seriousness of purpose."[14] In the Zurich production, by way of contrast, the sixth scene, in which Sophie incites the slum dwellers to arson, was cut. The farcical elements were emphasized, and although the audience heartily enjoyed the evening according to the critic Dieter Bachmann, the director had given Hochhuth a comedy by "misappropriating his anger."[15]

Once again, however, the major source of interest and controversy was the content of the play, rather than its form. Wolfgang Hochheim, head of the CDU in the Kiel government, reacted vehemently, because Hochhuth had also used Kiel as a specific example in the play. Even though the information Hochhuth gave had originally been printed in several magazine articles, only when it was included in the comedy did Hochheim object, deciding to sue Hochhuth for libel.[16] And certainly Hochhuth's position on the issue was best reflected by his use of such material, rather than by that of the comedy form. As in *Guerillas,* the dramaturgy was conventional. The most obvious change in *Die Hebamme* was Hochhuth's abandonment of the division into acts. Here instead we find eight *Bilder,* although the word was not used to refer to the presentation of simultaneous images or impressions. Hochhuth continued to develop a strictly linear plot. The first six scenes, which come before the intermission, involve the exposition and the plans for the arson, while the two longer scenes that follow show the aftermath in the hospital, where Sophie works as a midwife, and in the courtroom. A fairly strong cause-effect pattern emerges as the action proceeds from one *Bild* to the next.

Place is also treated in a realistic manner in *Die Hebamme.* Traditional settings were chosen for each *Bild,* and the tendency toward Realism was enhanced throughout by references to similar occurrences in the recent past, such as the following quotation inserted before the sixth scene: "Residents of a barracks village on the outskirts of Rome illegally occupied private buildings in Rome last week for the purpose of taking up residence. Afterwards, forced back to the slums, they destroyed their own housing with the objective of making themselves homeless. The city was thereby to be forced to provide them with new apartments" (H, 194).

Thus in this first comedy Hochhuth continued along a path already well defined by him in the 1960s. Despite a new political militancy, a concentration on contemporary issues, and the shift from tragedy to comedy, the basic *Weltanschauung* and the belief in the theater as a moral institution remained the same. As Hochhuth admitted, the use of comedy was perhaps the only way to make social criticism palatable to the larger public: "Social politics is a much too serious business to be treated without humor."[17] Whether *Die Hebamme* is, in fact, humorous is a question to be decided by the German audiences, which may or may not corroborate Karasek's dictum: "When Rolf Hochhuth and humor collide,the result is a dull thud."[18] *Newsweek* reported that Hochhuth's comedy had been "a resounding success," and it was indeed so with German audiences, if not with the critics. For several years, it was the most frequently performed play in West Germany.[19] Despite some evident weaknesses in its structure, as when the active heroine becomes suddenly inactive in the final scene — in spite of her advanced age her death seems particularly contrived — Hochhuth nevertheless had once again succeeded in bringing an important issue to the stage, in commanding the attention of his audiences, and in producing reactions well beyond the confines of the theater.

### III   Lysistrate und die Nato:
#### *The Female Versus the Male Principle*

It has been suggested that the box office success of *Die Hebamme* encouraged Hochhuth to write another comedy, but the author has denied such pecuniary motivation. As with his first comedy, the material had interested him for a long time; here the idea for the play even predated the composition of *The Deputy*. At the time of the premiere in Essen in February 1974, Hochhuth told the *Dramaturg* Fritz Gerhards that he had thought of using the Lysistrate material, modeled on the Aristophanes comedy, as early as 1957, but that at that time he had planned to locate the action in his native Hesse, close to the border of East Germany. "And it was supposed to deal with the refusal to give up farmland as a place for troop manoeuvers."[20] According to Hochhuth, it was Mrs. Piscator who first suggested moving the locale, perhaps even to Greece, when he was staying with her in New York at the time of the Broadway opening of *Soldiers*. And after writing *Die Hebamme,* the dramatist felt the need for a change of scene: "I wanted to work with an entirely new type of people, a new personnel, and for this reason I chose Greece as the setting of the new play."[21] Hochhuth's basic approach to comedy remained unchanged, however. *Lysistrate und die Nato* was also intended to teach a lesson, although the author specifically rejected the terms "documentary" or "political" drama: "People are tired today of being preached to from the stage. But if that is what is supposed to happen, and it is supposed to happen in my comedies, then it must be done through laughter."[22]

Hochhuth's *Lysistrate* follows much the same pattern as *Die Hebamme* in the interaction between its intent, its content, and its form. It uses comedy techniques, with a heroine as the main character, to reflect on an important contemporary problem — war. Hochhuth pictures a small Greek island, virtually unknown, although a former cabinet member makes his home there, whose farmers are about to sell their land so that a NATO air base can be built. They look forward to the new life that will be infused into the island's faltering economy. But the former school teacher, Lysistrate — now their representative in parliament — has a better idea. The new base, as she points out, would create an artificial boom, but it will not bring back the husbands who are forced to work abroad. In addition, it will endanger the inhabitants, as the recent death of two children during manoeuvers has presaged. Lysistrate persuades the wives of the farmers to use the age-old weapon that Aristophanes' women had used to bring about peace, for here too the peace of the island is potentially threatened. They agree to withhold themselves sexually from their husbands until the farmers are forced to give in and go along with Lysistrate's plan to make the island a tourist center.

Like Sophie, Lysistrate must use illegal means to reach this end. She blackmails the former minister so that he will underwrite the project, thus ironically using money which his company had siphoned off from the Greek defense budget. Lysistrate's dream of establishing a viable tourist center only becomes realizable, however, when the very military investigators who are checking the island's suitability for the NATO base discover a submerged statue of Aphrodite. Lysistrate steals the frogman's film, assuring that the discovery of this important work of art is publicized so as to make the island famous overnight, thus making it even less suitable as a secret landing site. The discovery of Aphrodite, in addition to serving this practical function in the plot, also symbolizes the ascendancy of the female principle in general. As Lysistrate says at the time of the discovery: "This find is a signal from Olympus as to who shall rule on this island!" (L, 92).

These intrigues are fully exposed in Acts I and II, which take place in the hotel owned by Lysistrate's father where the women are staying during their strike, as are the NATO officers. By the beginning of Act III, however, the sex strike seems to have become unnecessary, since all the men but one are now willing to accept the minister's money and Lysistrate's plan. At this point, Hochhuth's plot moves away from its original purpose. The strike has set these women free in a new way. They are learning to be independent by earning their own money through weaving. In addition, as part of the agreement, Lysistrate has arranged for them to become joint owners of the property. Changes in self-image are already apparent in the verbal abuse of the first act when one woman says, "Man, stop speaking of me as if I were your milk can, as if you could just take it or leave it" (L, 32). But as the women become more articulate and make the transition from servants to more liberated women, the repeated confrontations with their husbands, who appear in chorus like the Old Athenian men in Aristophanes' comedy, take on a logic of their own. In terms of the original goal of keeping NATO off the island, it makes little sense that the women are now sleeping with the officers, although it does have meaning as an expression of their new sexual freedom. To this Hochhuth adds the desire for revenge and the desire to torment (*Quälsucht*), which he considers a chiefly feminine attribute (see L, 143–44). Motivations for the action in Act IV are therefore provided, but in terms of the economy of the plot, the reaction of the women still seems grotesquely out of proportion.

It is interesting to contrast the sexual revolt depicted in *Lysistrate* with that portrayed in Aristophanes' comedy. In the Greek play the women are very conscious of being free citizens; they are therefore aware of their responsibility for the prosperity of the *polis* as well as for their own families. Despite the unusual nature of their action their motivation is clear-cut — they simply want peace. Oppression of women per se does not seem to play a role. The women have only a positive attitude toward their sexual relationships with men, and love is seen within the context of marriage as a source of fulfillment and happiness. The contemporary admonition, "make love not war," truly sums up the message of Aristophanes' comedy, as the women unite with the men in celebration of the whole pantheon at the end. The relationships between Hochhuth's women and their husbands are far more complicated and certainly less happy. Even when the real issue of the land seems to be solved, they do not want to return home. They want to use this opportunity to show the extent to which they despise, rather than love, their partners. At the same time, they also feel that they are being exploited by their new sexual partners.

In the end, the women and men conspire to assure the rapid departure of the NATO officers, which was inevitable at any rate. But in the background, more serious political events are unfolding that are referred to throughout the play. In the final scene, the Greek coup d'état is announced on the radio. Thus, despite her evident success in taming the farmers and assuring the ascendancy of Aphrodite on the island, Lysistrate is now faced with possible arrest by the military dictatorship and must go into hiding on Crete. It seems ironic that despite his previous praise of the strategy of coup d'état Hochhuth here criticizes it because of the supposed involvement of the CIA and the nature of the resulting dictatorship.

*Lysistrate und die Nato* combines the same elements of deadly seriousness of purpose with ribald comedy as did *Die Hebamme,* but far less successfully so. Hochhuth could not rely on dialect humor as in the first comedy, and often the dialogue is reduced to a recitation of clichés.[23] Comedy is introduced primarily by means of verbal and visual gags, like the fact that Lysistrate's father is hard of hearing and mixes things up, or that he takes his false teeth out on stage. Another visual gag, borrowed directly from Aristophanes, is the incident where the local religious leader, called the Pope, gets drenched with water (L, 119), only here it is an accident, whereas Aristophanes' Athenian women purposely doused the approaching firebrands. The obscenity in Aristophanes' play seems natural, whereas at times in Hochhuth's play it is forced and therefore embarassingly unfunny.[24] And despite the continued use of newspaper quotations at the beginning of each act to relate the action to current events, Hochhuth seems to have moved farther away from the "real" world. His island could be located anywhere, and the play resembles a parable, as he himself admitted in the introductory notes (L, 8). This rejection of the "realistic" element is confirmed by his statement of political purpose: "If comedy were as dreary as everyday life, it could not even make fun of our existence, for only through laughter can comedy fulfill its purpose, which is to make propaganda for the rational mind, that is, to engage in politics. And in that one can never succeed simply by imitating what already exists" (L, 9). But the final moments of the play are somber indeed, as the memory of Hitler is invoked. The minor success of Aphrodite's *Hetärismus* (promiscuity) is quickly overshadowed by the male principle of war.

Despite the great differences between Hochhuth and Aristophanes, it should be pointed out that they share a similar intent. Aristophanic comedy also had a moral and political purpose. It contained both comic and serious elements. As Alexis Solomos has noted in *The Living Aristophanes,* the technique can be compared to the works of some "engaged" writers of our own time, although he does not include Hochhuth in his list. Solomos points out that "comedy was not only a major theatrical entertainment but also the counterpart of modern journalism. The only form of social or political editorial the citizens could benefit by was the voice of the poet from the stage."[25] In addition, *Lysistrata* was written in 411 B.C. after the failure of the Sicilian invasion. The ribaldry was set against the audience's awareness of the reality of a lost war. And during that same year, an antidemocratic coup by the Four Hundred temporarily succeeded in creating an oligarchy in Athens. Allusions to the citizen's fear of such a takeover are to be found in the Greek comedy as well as in Hochhuth's play.

Yet despite this similarity in intention and in background, there could hardly be a greater contrast in the effect of the two plays. In commenting on Aristophanes' skill, Solomos has pointed out that "he knows how to restrain his personal feeling and to subdue every element of entertainment to the overall theatrical pattern; his own personality disappears behind the plot and the characters; he avoids even the sermon of the *parabasis,* having no hope of convincing the Athenians through direct admonition; his message is embodied in the play's action."[26] Exactly the contrary must be said of Hochhuth. All too often, as in *Guerillas,* his voice is heard through that of his main character. Lysistrate's speech in Act I is reminiscent of the arguments Hochhuth had presented in "Angst vor der 'Schutz'-Macht USA": "I am not a pacifist, after all. Doing without weapons does not protect one from them. We women reject the circumstance that foreigners make our island interesting to agressors under the guise of protecting Greece! No Russian would give our island a second glance — if the Americans did not 'give' us rockets. A great power, whose security is not *our* problem, wants to misuse our island as a lightning rod!" (L, 61).

Furthermore, Hochhuth was not able to embody his message in the play's action, because it went beyond the simple appeal for peace which had characterized Aristophanes' play. Instead he found it necessary to append an essay entitled "Frauen und Mütter, Bachofen und Germaine Greer" ("Women and Mothers...") in order to score his point. In it he shows with what utter seriousness he regards the "comic" revolt carried out on this little island. The essay provides a rather remarkable contribution to Hochhuth's political theories and demonstrates his peculiar brand of male chauvinism.

Hochhuth in fact rejects the very idea of equality of the sexes. The women's liberation movement, he feels, has only resulted in an even more slavish imitation of men by women, although that is due in part to the "Kopistennatur der Frau" ("copyist nature of woman," [L, 297]). The author introduces his main points in the form of rhethorical questions. "Do they read history unless the man they love is reading it, because they want to talk with him 'about everything,' even if they have little interest in it?'' (L, 202). According to him, a few women in the literary field have escaped this copyist nature and have succeeded in writing feminine (*weibliche*) plays and novels (L, 197).

Hochhuth emphasizes the importance of motherhood, as the title of the essay suggests: "In what other way have women achieved anything exceptional?" (L, 199). He further asks: "Are women pioneers in any direction at all? For example, to a land that they want to establish themselves from the ground up? Could they even achieve the requisite solidarity with each other? Have they, up to now, been able to develop solidarity, which has not been sacrificed to a man as soon as they loved him?" (L, 204). Without directly answering these rhetorical questions, Hochhuth does suggest that the answer is "no." At the same time, he feels that women have only themselves to blame and not men. He finds entering previously male-dominated professions like law or medicine, even the military, an absurd goal for women. For in so doing they will give up their one great advantage, being "other" than men. "What on earth would be changed (or even improved) if women came to resemble those who have polluted the world and encumbered history? Why seek those rights with which men have institutionalized suffering?" (L, 205). The author ignores his previous admonition, however, for how can women be expected to bring about the revolution he envisions without becoming part of the ruling oligarchy?

While criticizing women, on the one hand, for not being independent enough to develop an alternate vision of the world, Hochhuth still seems to think that they may be the only force that can save the world by speaking directly to the two key problems of poverty and war. For he interprets these as problems created by the domination of the male principle. He uses the dichotomy outlined by Bachofen in his *Mutterrecht,* but insists on the need to return from the *Vaterrecht* of Roman law to a female principle based on the *Hetärismus* of Aphrodite. He also cites Germaine Greer, who, he feels, supports his notion that women must seek a model in opposition to the world of men instead of an access to it.[27] But whenever Hochhuth approaches the all-important question of means, he sidesteps the issue: "Since I am not a woman I cannot know, and even women have not as yet discovered how" (L, 217). At the same time, he does indicate, in the essay as well as in the comedy, that women have at least one effective weapon. They must use the force of Eros to change the world. The example set by Lysistrate is to be taken quite literally as a kind of passive resistance to which active means must be joined — suggestions are lacking — "in a manner which makes men as vulnerable as they are completely surprised" (L, 217). Sex is thus explored by Hochhuth as a potential revolutionary tactic. "Licentiousness in the erotic realm is the *only* means for a woman to escape being reined in by man" (L, 233). What seems particularly surprising about this essay is the indication that women ought to seek the very utopia which Hochhuth had found so distasteful when discovered by men. But as the comedy shows, this utopia can only exist on an island, in isolation, whereas back on the mainland the military takeover assures the continuance of the male principle of war and power politics, thereby providing the ultimate tragic contrast to the comic interlude.

The reactions to *Lysistrate und die Nato* were again mixed. It was, like *Die Hebamme,* more easily accepted by audiences than critics. The play opened on February 22, 1974, at the Viennese Volkstheater under the direction of Peter Lotschak, and in Essen under the direction of Erich Schumacher. By the end of the 1973–1974 season, *Lysistrate und die Nato* had already been seen by more than forty-eight thousand people in eighty-three performances of three different productions. *Die Hebamme* came in a close second in the theater statistics, recording five different productions and one hundred and three performances seen by over forty-six thousand theatergoers.[28] In the theatrical journals, however, there was an almost embarassed silence about this play, a refusal to take Hochhuth's comedy seriously. Hellmuth Karasek used the Essen premiere as an occasion for more namecalling. Hochhuth, he said in a review that appeared in *Der Spiegel,* is "a Schiller in suspenders." He accused the dramatist of being "provincial, unsophisticated and a secret male fanatic." Yet faced with the evident popularity of *Die Hebamme,* the most frequently performed play of the previous season, he came to the conclusion that he must resign himself to the fact that Hochhuth had an uncanny sense for "giving philistine banalities the appearance of progressive provocation."[29] By way of contrast, when *Lysistrate und die Nato* opened at the Volkstheater in Rostock in December, under the direction of Hanns Anselm Perten, the reviewer exaggerated the significance of the comedy, calling it an "important contribution to our mastery over the present."[30] This praise can only be understood in light of the fact that the East Germans were able to interpret the play as an attack on American imperialism.

Certainly neither of these assessments can be accepted at face value. Although *Lysistrate und die Nato* had a definite appeal to audiences in both West and East Germany, it is marred by inconsistencies in the plot and by its reliance on verbal and visual gags for the comic effect. The comedy and its accompanying essay are nonetheless interesting as reflections of Hochhuth's development as an engaged author after 1970. In fact, both *Die Hebamme* and *Lysistrate und die Nato* — whatever their individual deficiencies — do reveal that Hochhuth, without changing course, had nevertheless come half-circle in his dramaturgy from the "realistic" historical tragedy, *The Deputy,* to a parablelike tragicomedy, *Lysistrate.* Such a development suggests that the critic must reassess the relationship of Hochhuth's dramaturgy — after the shift to comedy — to Dürrenmatt's concept of the tragicomic. In addition, Hochhuth's choice of Sisyphus as a symbolic figure at this particular point in his development suggests that a reconsideration of Hochhuth's relationship to the Theater of the Absurd is likewise in order.

### IV   Hochhuth, Dürrenmatt, Camus: The Realistic, the Grotesque, and the Absurd

At the very beginning of his dramatic career, Hochhuth had explicitly countered the contention that tragic heroes no longer exist in contemporary society. Of those who asserted that "pure tragedy" was no longer possible — and there were several including Adorno — Friedrich Dürrenmatt proffered an important statement of this position in his *Theaterprobleme.* In this 1954 essay, the Swiss dramatist specifically rejected the Schillerian aesthetics and the historical drama which Hochhuth later embraced, arguing that comedy, with its use of the grotesque, was the only form "suitable for us" today.[31]

The world today as it appears to us could hardly be encompassed in the form of the historical drama as Schiller wrote it, for the reason alone that we no longer have any tragic heroes, but only vast tragedies staged by world butchers and produced by slaughtering machines.... Schiller's drama presupposes a world that the eye can take in, that takes for granted genuine actions of state, just as Greek tragedy did. The state today, however, cannot be envisioned, for it is anonymous and bureaucratic; and not only in Moscow and Washington, but also in Berne. Actions of state today have become *post-hoc* satyric dramas which follow the tragedies executed in secret earlier. True representatives of our world are missing; the tragic heroes are nameless. Any small-time crook, petty government official or policeman better represents our world than a senator or president.[32]

Hochhuth's position in 1963 seemed to be diametrically opposed to that expressed by Dürrenmatt. The author of *The Deputy* specifically named the Swiss playwright as an opponent when he insisted, in defense of his first drama, that tragedy was still possible, that individual leaders still made decisions for which they were then responsible.[33] Hochhuth refuses to believe that there are no longer genuine acts of state, that our modern tragedies are of such complexity, so devoid of meaning, and so abstract as to defy explanation by or portrayal through the medium of tragedy. He purposely chose a Pope, a prime minister, and a senator, if not a president, as the key figures in his three tragedies. But in turning to comedy Hochhuth seemed to have abandoned his original position in favor of Dürrenmatt's world of the "small-time crook or petty government official." But Hochhuth's selection, in *Die Hebamme* and *Lysistrate und die Nato,* of characters from the ordinary run of life did not imply that he thought of them as "better" representatives of our world. Hochhuth's use of the comedy form, as we have already noted, did not mean a rejection of his previous position. For him comedy simply could provide another way of portraying our world, but not the only possible one, as Dürrenmatt's statement implies.

Yet we ought not overlook the similarity between what Hochhuth was now trying to achieve through his comedies and the description Dürrenmatt gave in *Theaterprobleme* of the role of comedy. It would be wrong to think of these two dramatists as continuing to represent opposites, at least in terms of their intent. In the interview with Gerhards Hochhuth had revealed that his reason for turning to comedy was that he was convinced it would be more effective than tragedy in gaining the public's attention.[34] Dürrenmatt had emphasized in *Theaterprobleme* that comedy could act like a trap: "The conceit easily transforms the crowd of theatre-goers into a mass which can be attacked, deceived, outsmarted into listening to things it would otherwise not so readily listen to. Comedy is a mousetrap in which the public is easily caught and in which it will

get caught over and over again."[35] Thus for both Hochhuth and
Dürrenmatt comedy was a way of disguising a serious purpose.
What was presented in a harmless way was, in fact, a potentially
dangerous weapon, "an art that exposes, demands, moralizes."
Dürrenmatt warned, however, that this fact must not be revealed
by a moralizing tone, for as soon as this is recognized, the play will
be "dropped like a hot potato, for art may be everything it wants to
be so long as it remains *gemütlich*."[36] Indeed, this may be the problem that Hochhuth has encountered with the critics.

There is another striking similarity between the theoretical position of Dürrenmatt as expressed in this essay and Hochhuth's use
of comedy; that is, the extent to which the tragic is considered an
essential component. Dürrenmatt insisted that while "pure tragedy" was no longer possible, "we can achieve the tragic out of
comedy. We can bring it forth as a frightening moment, as an abyss
that opens suddenly."[37] In Hochhuth's comedies, however, the
tragic element serves as a kind of static, somber backdrop, rather
than growing directly out of the comic situation as Dürrenmatt suggests here. For instance, in *Lysistrate* the announcement of the
coup at the conclusion is not surprising or shocking, for hints
throughout the play have prepared the audience for this event,
which, in addition, is set entirely apart from the dramatic action,
rather than arising organically out of it.

Despite some basic similarities in their attitude toward comedy,
Dürrenmatt's theory and practice differ markedly from those of
Hochhuth in a number of important respects, as for example in his
attitude toward time, place, and characterization. Hochhuth used
linear time and realistic place in his comedies in a way that differed
little from his approach in the tragedies. Dürrenmatt, on the other
hand, although he guarded against pure abstraction, had a more
experimental attitude toward the use of time and place. He rejected
the kind of verisimilitude that Hochhuth's scenic notes seem to require of the stage sets. In his play *Die Ehe des Herrn Mississippi
(The Marriage of Mr. Mississippi),* which he specifically uses as an
example in *Theaterprobleme,* he wanted to experiment with the
concept of "indefiniteness of the locale."[38] Although the room was
to seem "real," it was not to represent a location in the traditional
sense. The right window looks out on a northern landscape, while
the left one looks out on a southern exposure. And during the
course of the play this room "disintegrates," revealing the abyss of

the tragic. While allowing for the realistic on the one hand, Dürren-matt was continually exploring the grotesque on the other. This is also true of his characters. Thus Claire Zachanassian in *Der Besuch der alten Dame (The Visit),* although on the surface she appears to be a real individual, is actually a conglomerate of false teeth, hair, and artificial limbs. For Hochhuth, however, there is never any question of the reality of his places, of time, or of his characters, even when the latter are stereotyped. *Lysistrate und die Nato* comes closest to escaping historical, if not linear time, but even here the oblique references to the 1967 Greek coup tie the comic action to a specific historical event.

With respect to the development of a dramatic action, however, Dürrenmatt and Hochhuth are far closer than might be assumed, for both see the need for dramatic tension and conflict. Without it, Dürrenmatt insisted, there could be no dramatic dialogue. While allowing for the use of monologue in his plays, Dürrenmatt, like Hochhuth, gave dialogue the greatest importance in the develop-ment of a plot: "Just as dialogue must develop out of a situation, so it must also lead into some situation, that is to say, of course, a new situation. Dramatic dialogue effects some action, some suffer-ing, some new situation, out of which in turn new dialogue can again develop, and so on and so forth."[39] Thus Dürrenmatt also relied on a dramatic cause-effect pattern rather than on the descrip-tion of a static situation.

What distinguishes Dürrenmatt from Hochhuth in his under-standing of the world and of comedy is his position on the crucial question of responsibility. Dürrenmatt rejected "pure tragedy" be-cause it presupposed guilt as well as responsibility. And for him "there are no more guilty, and also no responsible, men."[40] Hoch-huth would still vehemently disagree on this point, even after the turn to comedy that apparently brought him closer to Dürrenmatt's position. For him, individuals are still accountable for their actions; he simply carried over his belief in the ultimate responsibil-ity of each individual into the realm of comedy. Thus there is not such a great difference between his heroine Sophie in *Die Hebamme* and the tragic hero of *Guerillas,* Senator Nicolson. In one case, the individual revolt is apparently successful, in the other apparently unsuccessful.

Yet despite these basic differences in the form and content of their plays, both playwrights suggest that all is not lost. Even in an absurd world one should not despair. As Dürrenmatt puts it:

After all this the conclusion might easily be drawn that comedy is the expression of despair, but this conclusion is not inevitable. To be sure, whoever realizes the senselessness, the hopelessness of this world might well despair, but this despair is not a result of this world. Rather it is an answer given by an individual to this world; another answer would be not to despair, would be an individual's decision to endure this world in which we live like Gulliver among the giants. He also achieves distance, he also steps back a pace or two who takes measure of his opponent, who prepares himself to fight his opponent or to escape him. It is still possible to show man as a courageous being.[41]

Although Dürrenmatt did not use the figure of Sisyphus to symbolize this kind of "courageous being," he might very well have done so. Like Hochhuth's Sisyphus, the Gulliver of whom he speaks is an individual who does not despair but endures. Thus despite his appreciation for the absurdity of our world and the grotesque element in our response to it, Dürrenmatt also allowed for some positive movement. In this case, however, it is described not as forward motion but as a stepping backward to gain distance, as the preparation for a struggle or escape. It could be compared to the attitude of "lucidity" which Camus emphasized in *The Myth of Sisyphus* as a prerequisite for absurd activity.[42] Hochhuth emphasized the next step, in which the courageous being moves the rock up the hill, despite the fact that he knows that such an effort will be self-defeating. But it is nevertheless here that we find the true link between Dürrenmatt's tragicomedy and Hochhuth's comedy. In both, the playwrights are trying to express in the form of a dramatic action the absurdity of existence on the one hand, and the dignity of man who endures — even strives in the face of it — on the other. Despite major differences in their techniques and in their basic understanding of the individual's guilt and responsibility, both Dürrenmatt and Hochhuth feel it is their task as dramatists to "demonstrate freedom."[43] Hochhuth called it the "struggle to realize our idea of freedom, our Sisyphus game" (K, 95). But both playwrights wanted to help heave the stone, and Hochhuth revealed with his turn to comedy that like Dürrenmatt, he found parody and satire useful tools in the struggle. Dürrenmatt, however, considered them to be the only effective ones, and moved beyond parody to the grotesque, a step Hochhuth was unwilling to take.

Hochhuth's choice of Sisyphus as a symbolic figure at this point in his development raises another question of comparison: How does Hochhuth's view of this mythical figure differ from the interpretation of Camus, and what will similarities and differences reveal about Hochhuth's understanding of the absurd and his relationship to the Theater of the Absurd? Hochhuth had earlier described the Theater of the Absurd as the opposite of his "Realistic Theater." His reason for this evaluation was, in fact, quite similar to his rejection of Dürrenmatt's view of tragedy, for the Absurd writers also did not believe in the guilt and responsibility of the individual. Hochhuth saw it as his task to reinstate the individual in his rightful position. "*That* is, after all, the essential task of drama: to insist that man is a responsible being" (H, 319). It is significant that here Hochhuth does not differentiate between tragedy and comedy. The fact that he republished his important theoretical statement, "Soll das Theater die heutige Welt darstellen?" in the volume containing his first comedy is one more indication that his turn to comedy and his new emphasis on the absurd did not contradict his earlier comments. In the 1963 essay he had already pointed out that his approach was not inconsistent with an appreciation of the absurd. Yet at that time he showed little understanding of the comic. He felt that caricature would only weaken his "realistic" approach. Our reaction to the absurdity of history should be shock and horror, and it should not be subdued through laughter. He therefore criticized Brecht's *Arturo Ui* and Chaplain's *Great Dictator* on the grounds that they made fun of something that was terrifying: "Treiben sie nicht nur mit Entsetzen Scherz?" (H, 324).

But despite this apparent aversion to humor, Hochhuth's world view had allowed for the absurd. What the introduction of the Sisyphus figure added was simply a new symbol by means of which Hochhuth could better concentrate on the issue that had been of greatest importance to him from the beginning; that is, the correct response of the individual to our world. Hochhuth was searching for a hero of humanist affirmation who could become his symbol for the politically active person in revolt against authority. He wanted a hero who would embody the kind of personal revolt which provided the only meaningful response to a seemingly hostile and indifferent world.

Hochhuth's interpretation of Sisyphus seems to coincide in many respects with that of Camus in *The Myth of Sisyphus,* although the German playwright, unlike the French Existentialist, did not devote an entire essay to this figure. Nevertheless, both writers emphasize that Sisyphus represents only one possible attitude of the individual toward his existence — not despair, but absurd striving. Camus defines the other alternative very precisely as suicide, an alternative that Hochhuth was to explore in his next major drama, *Tod eines Jägers (Death of a Hunter),* which depicts the suicide of Ernest Hemingway. Hochhuth's sense of moral outrage over the horrors of our past and present history might be called that "discomfort in the face of man's own inhumanity" which Camus called the definition of the absurd attitude.[44] Camus, like Hochhuth, rejected final goals and ultimate solutions, but he found hope in the defiance expressed by Sisyphus; his permanent revolution carried into individual experience seemed to give "life its value."[45] But there is a clear difference between Camus and Hochhuth nonetheless. Camus could not accept the traditional concepts of guilt and responsibility; thus the difference between these two authors parallels that between Dürrenmatt and Hochhuth. Although all three in fact choose hope rather than indifference, although they all stress the importance of lucidity in face of the absurd reality, only Hochhuth clings to the "truth in history" which he feels renders it possible to make moral judgments. Despite his awareness of the absurd, he thus aligns himself with what Camus called "the classical sensibility," which concentrated on moral rather than metaphysical issues.[46] In this sense, Hochhuth is classical rather than modern, for even after the turn to comedy, he is still primarily concerned with moral issues. And while he seems to agree with Camus' description of the absurd and of Sisyphus' affirming role, his drama has no similarity with the so-called "Theater of the Absurd." Perhaps his partial alignment with Camus helps to explain this fact. In drawing a distinction between writers of the Theater of the Absurd on the one hand, and Existentialist writers, like Camus, on the other, Martin Esslin has pointed out that they are using two entirely different conventions. The latter

present their sense of the irrationality of the human condition in the form of highly lucid and logically constructed reasoning, while the Theater of the Absurd strives to express its sense of the senselessness of the human condition and the inadequacy of the rational approach by the open abandonment of rational devices and discursive thought. While Sartre or Camus express the new content in the old convention, the Theatre of the Absurd goes a step further in trying to achieve a unity between its basic assumptions and the form in which they are expressed.[47]

Hochhuth certainly shares with Camus the reliance on conventional modes of discursive thought, both in his essays and dramas, but what is an apparent paradox in the case of Camus remains logically consistent in that of Hochhuth, because he does not accept all of the basic assumptions behind the absurd position. While insisting on the absurd quality of history, the cyclical patterns of "progress," Hochhuth remains faithful to the concept of guilt and responsibility on the part of the individual. Thus his choice of traditional conventions, either in tragedy or comedy, is a coherent expression of his world view. A rejection of his dramaturgy implies a rejection of his *Weltanschauung,* as was clearly demonstrated by the Adorno controversy. Thus, despite a certain lip service to the absurd, Hochhuth's dramatic form is in fact diametrically opposed to the Theater of the Absurd. Whereas the latter "cannot show the clash of opposing temperaments or study human passion locked in conflict,"[48] Hochhuth builds his dramaturgy on just such conflicts. Whereas the Theater of the Absurd lacks objectively valid characters, Hochhuth continues to present them. Whereas the Theater of the Absurd explores static situations, Hochhuth continues to rely on linear plot development. Whereas the Theater of the Absurd puts language itself into question, Hochhuth accepts language as a vehicle of communication.[49] And whereas the Theater of the Absurd is not "concerned with telling a story in order to communicate some moral or social lesson,"[50] Hochhuth's purpose is exactly that. Although Hochhuth did choose an absurd image in Sisyphus, he nevertheless emphasized in his two comedies the positive side of Sisyphus' paradoxical situation, i.e., the possibility of individual remedial revolutionary action in the face of injustice. But with the choice of suicide as the theme of his next major drama, he indicated that the absurdity of all human endeavor in the face of death is never quite forgotten. His conception of life remained at the same time comic and deeply tragic.

CHAPTER 7

# Monologues of Resignation

I    *Justice and Judges:* Juristen

AT the time of the premiere of *Lysistrate und die Nato* in Essen, Hochhuth was already announcing the theme and title of his next play. The setting was to be the Federal Republic of Germany, the country that had always received his closest scrutiny and most scathing criticism. The time was to be the 1960s, but the perspective of the past was to be provided by action that took place in Poland in 1943. Hochhuth said of the play, *Juristen,* then in progress, that "it is a very sad piece. It deals with the question to what extent the biblical words which Theodor Heuss used at the founding of the Federal Republic, namely, 'justice elevates a people,' to what extent this saying of our first president has actually been realized in our state."[1] The topic of justice and judges was not entirely new to Hochhuth, and thus it was no surprise that he should try to give it an appropriate dramatic form. His ballad, "Juristen," one of the rhymed commentaries in "Deutschland braucht Bayern," had indicated the cynicism with which Hochhuth viewed the many judges who had been able to make such an easy transition from Nazi Germany to the Federal Republic, as well as his criticism of the government which had so often awarded them handsome pensions: "nicht einer ward vor Gericht gestellt,/ der für die Schänder des Vaterlands,/ für die Nazis — die Todesurteile gefällt" ("Not one of them was brought to trial,/ who pronounced the death sentences/ for the Nazis — for the violators of the fatherland" [H, 308]).

The corruption of justice in West Germany had also been a key issue in *Die Hebamme,* and Sister Sophie had contrasted her misdeeds to the criminality of German judges — even the law itself: "I ask you: what is a personal infraction in comparison to our criminal code? We live in a republic whose highest judge recently retired — and only because of pressure from abroad — with a pension of two thousand eight hundred marks a month, because he had nearly fifty people beheaded under Hitler. The highest judge of this state! Measure that criminality of our officialdom against my offenses against this criminality" (H, 182). Sophie also refers to the biblical quote cited by Theodor Heuss at the time of the founding of the Federal Republic, and she reveals Hochhuth's probable answer to the question he intended to raise in *Juristen*. For according to her this maxim has never been realized in West Germany because the government has used the word "justice" as a blindfold for the people (H, 183).

For whatever reason, *Juristen* has not yet been published.[2] Instead, Hochhuth's next drama, *Tod eines Jägers,* which appeared in April 1976, turned away from the revolt against authority symbolized by Sisyphus to an exploration of the other alternative suggested by Camus and Dürrenmatt — despair, resignation, escape, and suicide. Although this was Hochhuth's first drama to deal exclusively with the theme of death, it was not a new topic for him either, since a reflection on death had gone hand in hand with his deep concern for the meaning of life. In *The Deputy,* Hochhuth's fictional hero, Riccardo, had searched for this meaning in the death camp of Auschwitz. The last act of the drama was subtitled with the question: "Where are you, God?" The sinister doctor, who called himself "the lord of life and death in this place" (De, 238), confronted Riccardo with his brand of nihilism and forced the priest to ask the question of whether life or death had any meaning in Auschwitz. It is significant for tracing Hochhuth's development from a drama of ideas based on dialogue to the monodrama of resignation, *Tod eines Jägers,* to note that Hochhuth had used monologues at the beginning of this act in order to set the mood for the contemplation of death. But the actual confrontation takes place in dialogue form, in the discussion between the doctor and Riccardo (De, 244–55).

In his second drama, *Soldiers,* the theme of death was also raised. It is important that Hochhuth subtitled the drama a *Nekrolog,* a form that he has often used to pay tribute to the dead.[3] But here the figure of death in the form of the burned woman of Dresden appeared only in the framework, and here too, the monologue played only a minor role. Unlike Riccardo, Dorland must confront this symbol of death without God, for he feels in a world without universal values that all that is left is death itself: "I usually write by the open window. My desk is so placed that the dark glass of the window, in front of the gray wall, reflects my own image — depressing. Each time I look in that black pane of glass, I see the portrait of the pilot. How easy it must formerly have been ... to live, to kill, as easy as for the medieval Everyman: One laid one's charge on God — and died discharged. Today — today, the only partner left for us is Death" (S, 24). These words could have been part of a monologue, but they are addressed to the sculptor. Dorland slips only occasionally into the traditional soliloquy. For the most part, he must converse with dream figures in his *Gewissensprozeß* (trial of conscience) in order to preserve at least the semblance of dialogue. But this passage does reveal an interesting direct link to *Tod eines Jägers.* In the monodrama, the author, Hemingway, also stands in front of just such a black pane of glass, a window like the one Dorland mentions here. He can see himself, his wasted frame and aging countenance, but he can also see figures from the past (T, 16–17). Here too, the black mirror is "depressing." As Hochhuth pointed out in *Soldiers,* the black glass has always symbolized melancholy in Western art (S, 24).

Although Hochhuth had also used the monologue form briefly during the second act of *Guerillas* (G, 109–10), this technique played virtually no role at all in his third drama or in the two comedies to follow. And despite the death of both Nicolson and Sophie, the contemplation of death is less important than in the first two plays. Hochhuth's return to this theme and the exclusive use of monologue in *Tod eines Jägers* seem all the more remarkable because of his earlier insistence that dramatic tension demands a conflict of ideas expressed through dialogue. Only now, in the text of the monodrama, does he indicate agreement with the position of Gottfried Benn, from whom he quotes: "'In der Tat: nur im Monolog spricht sich der Dualismus, die Antithese, das Drama von heute aus'" ("'Indeed: only in the monologue does the dualism, the antithesis, the drama of today find expression'" [T, 40]). But Hochhuth had experimented more fully with the monologue form and with the theme of resignation and death in several of his short stories, which, although less well known than his dramas, are also deserving of our attention.

## II  *"Kleine Prosa": Minor Prose Works*

Hochhuth included several short stories in the *Hebamme* collection of 1971 under the heading "Kleine Prosa." I shall briefly consider two of them because of the extent to which they reveal Hochhuth's concern with the possibility of despair and resignation as the other response to life's absurdity. *Die Berliner Antigone,* a novella written in 1961, was first performed in 1966.[4] It is a story of classical simplicity based on a documented account from the year 1943 and told in the third person. A young girl steals her brother's body after his hanging and buries the corpse illegally. The judge who presides over Anne's trial is ironically the father of her fiancé, Bodo, but he is unable to turn the tragedy into a farce (H, 41). Anne refuses to deny the act, although no one can prove that she is responsible. She is convicted and sentenced to death. But as she awaits her execution, she no longer understands her "heroic" act. It no longer seems to have any meaning, and she does not recognize herself. She has to admit to herself her fear of death, which she does not even share with Bodo: "She dared not reveal to him how hopeless she felt" (H, 45). After Bodo commits suicide at the front, thinking Anne already dead, she resigns herself to her fate. But the narrator reveals no sense of victory here; her execution seems to be totally senseless.

Another story written even earlier is of greater interest to us because of its experimentation with the monologue form in conjunction with the theme of resignation. Written in 1959, it was first published in *Die Hebamme* under the title "Resignation oder die Geschichte einer Ehe" ("Resignation, or the story of a marriage"). Then, after Hochhuth's divorce from his wife Marianne in 1972, he returned to this work and rewrote it in 1974 for publication under the title *Zwischenspiel in Baden-Baden.* Despite the change in title, the original diary form was retained, and the theme of resignation continued to play a central role. A middle-aged woman discovers that her husband is having an affair with a teenager. She walks out on him and takes her two children for several weeks' vacation to the resort town of Baden-Baden in order to think things over. There she gets legal advice and personal comfort from a new acquaintance, Hilmes. But the diary in which she reflects on her past, present, and possible future is far more decisive than Hilmes' entertaining comments about marriage in bringing her to the point where she prefers to return to her husband rather than risk an affair with the lawyer-friend. In fact, she chooses the path of least resistance; it is a form of resignation, for she is basically afraid that she could not cope with a change in lifestyle, although she feels that her marriage is unsatisfactory. She is also fearful that her doctor-husband may be correct in maintaining that too much self-scrutiny is dangerous. "'Self-awareness sounds very nice — but in reality it is self-dissection, and that promotes suicide in all those who already have a tendency to consult psychiatrists'" (Z, 41). What she fears most, however, is approaching old age — the prospect of being alone. When she finally makes the decision to return home, it is not with a sense of victory but of defeat because of her dependence. As a sign of her ultimate resignation she also abandons her diary, her only channel for creativity and self-expression.

The reworking of this prose piece in 1974 gave Hochhuth a chance to use the extended monologue form before applying it to a dramatic situation in *Tod eines Jägers*. The story line of *Zwischenspiel* is essentially the same as in "Resignation," but Hochhuth lengthened the story considerably, allowing the woman to launch into reflections not only on her own situation and her past, but on the world around her, covering subjects ranging from architecture to education. To a certain extent, the characters of the wife and the husband in this story of a marriage are then combined in Hochhuth's Hemingway figure. The American author as Hochhuth depicted him combines the active and contemplative roles. He reflects on his past, present, and imminent future — his suicide — in the same way as this woman, but this contemplative approach is terribly painful for him because all his life he had avoided such self-dissection in favor of the escapist approach of the husband. Hochhuth clearly states that "our old man can, for good reason, be included among the active and among the contemplative types" (T, 83). In *Tod eines Jägers* Hochhuth also continued to explore the possible link between old age, loneliness, and suicide that he had introduced in *Zwischenspiel* with the following statement: "Fear of old age is fear — a very justified one — of being alone.... Old people, alone within their four walls, make up the largest number of suicides" (Z, 145).

### III   Tod eines Jägers: *A Monodrama of Suicide*

At the very beginning of *The Myth of Sisyphus* Camus had stated that "there is but one truly serious philosophical problem, and that is suicide."[5] This essay was in fact Camus' attempt to resolve that problem, and his answer was clear: "Even if one does not believe in God, suicide is not legitimate."[6] Hochhuth's choice of Sisyphus as a model for man's individual response to the world would suggest agreement with Camus' conclusion. But like the French Existentialist writer, Hochhuth found it necessary to inquire into the relationship between individual thought and suicide. What leads a man to take this step? What leads him, as Camus put it, "from lucidity in the face of existence to flight from light?"[7] *Tod eines Jägers,* a monodrama dealing with the imagined thoughts of Ernest Hemingway during the last hours before his suicide, gives Hochhuth's answer to this question. In the play he concentrates, above all, on the fate of Hemingway the writer. Hochhuth had showed his concern for the plight of aging writers in "Unsere 'abgeschriebenen' Schriftsteller in der Bundesrepublik" (H, 335–46). In this 1970 appeal Hochhuth concurred with the position of Gottfried Benn that the stress situation in which all aging people find themselves is particularly difficult and brutal in the case of artists because of the spiritual isolation that they experience (H, 340–41).[8] But Hochhuth went even further and speculated whether this could explain the high percentage of suicides among writers (H, 341).

Hochhuth had thus been concerned with the problem of suicide among authors in at least a general way for some time before writing the monodrama, a typical phenomenon with all his plays. There is also some indication that he had been reading Hemingway at the time of writing *Lysistrate und die Nato,* since he specifically used the American novelist as a reference in the accompanying essay, "Frauen und Mütter..." (L, 226).[9] And Hochhuth was not the only contemporary dramatist to use this subject. After 1970 the death of writers and old age in general had become popular topics for plays.[10] The most interesting comparison can be made with Tankred Dorst's *Eiszeit (Ice Age,* 1973), a drama based on the last years of another aging author, the Norwegian novelist Knut Hamsun. Hamsun was accused of being a traitor to his country during the Nazi period, yet the old man of Dorst's play — already in his nineties — is still defiant, very much alive, as he says at the end: "Ja, ja, ja, ich lebe noch!" ("Yes, yes, yes, I'm still alive!").[11] Although he feels himself to be misunderstood, although he is estranged from society, he remains testy and tenacious, and he states more in defiance than resignation: "I am dead! As an author I am dead! ... I have been sitting on my farm for the last thirty years, old, deaf, and dead!"[12] The accusations that he must face, however, come from without, not from within, and it is the young man, Oswald, who commits suicide. The contrast to Hochhuth's Hemingway is striking. Here a defeated sixty year old looks and acts much older than he is. He has developed a characteristic gesture of resignation (T, 22), and his accusations are self-inflicted and therefore self-destructive.

Hochhuth had evidently studied the important biographies of Hemingway, as well as the American author's works, since he uses many quotations from the novels in the monodrama; and he rests his interpretation of Hemingway's final mental illness on the accounts by A. E. Hotchner and Carlos Baker (T, 10).[13] He also seems to have been familiar with the assessment of Gregory H. Hemingway, the author's youngest son, who in his memoir published in 1976 indicated that it was primarily the loss of creativity which had motivated his father's suicide shortly after his release from the Mayo clinic in July 1961. The son maintained that his father simply could not endure the pain accompanying the loss of talent, which had begun to ebb nearly a decade before: "He always had a marvelous ear for words and he was certainly more experienced and wiser, but the old effortless elemental naturalness was no longer there. The world no longer flowed through him as through a purifying filter, with the distillate seeming more true and beautiful than the world itself. He was no longer a poet, one of God's spies, but a querulous counterespionage agent whose operatives seemed to deceive him."[14] Gregory also stressed the fact that his father's whole philosophy of life with its emphasis on physical vigor would not allow him to accept old age with dignity. Thus it was a combination of mental and physical feebleness at the early age of sixty-one, as well as the inability to write, that made Hemingway choose the only escape left to him. But the son interprets this decision positively: "I think he showed courage in accepting the only option left."[15]

Although Hochhuth remained basically faithful to this and other biographical accounts of Hemingway's last days in his home in Ketchum, Idaho, depicting the author's paranoia, and his conviction that the IRS was pursuing him and that his most trusted friends — even his wife Mary — were part of the conspiracy, the monodrama is still a creation of Hochhuth's imagination. It is clear that such a death scene cannot be "documentary." The monodrama also reflects Hochhuth's concerns about the role of the writer in society, perhaps more so than those of the author about whom he was ostensibly writing. And although Hochhuth referred to Hemingway as a "hunter" in the title of the play, it is the author Hemingway who is at center stage: "The fact that the old man had to die when he could no longer write — or imagined himself incapable — proves that he was first and foremost an author and only incidentally a hunter, for he could still have continued to fish or hunt" (T, 84). Despite such a comment in the stage directions, the use of the word *Jäger* in the title of the play is quite appropriate; he is tracking himself down relentlessly until he finally pulls the trigger to put the exhausted animal out of its misery.

While emphasizing the loss of Hemingway's creative powers as the main reason for his suicide, Hochhuth also explores the degree to which fear was a catalyst throughout Hemingway's life, and not only an experience of the final moments:

His obsessive need to be a champion, to catch the heaviest marlin and to hunt the biggest horned antelope, can only have been rooted in fear: fear of imagined personal weaknesses and fear also as citizen of a nation that had reverted to the wanton destructiveness of its early history by dropping the atomic bomb. Even though the old man was probably at that time the most respected person in the USA next to the President, he never spoke out against the bombings publicly.... War only interested him when he could participate as a crack soldier. (T, 12)

This passage from the introductory notes combines Hochhuth's analysis of the individual human being with an identification of this man and his country. It is a phenomenon which recurs throughout the play. Hochhuth portrays Hemingway as a man of his time who exemplifies the guilt of his generation. He thus goes beyond a simple exploration of the suicide to examine Hemingway's life and works, measuring them against his ideal of the engaged author. But through the medium of monologue, this critical analysis becomes self-criticism, and thus, within the monodrama, it helps to motivate the final action of the character.

Hochhuth's Hemingway looks back at his life and ruthlessly rejects most of it: "The journalist in me is at fault for hardly having an eye for the ordinary, but only for the sensational and for the

privileged few to whom I belonged'' (T, 57). In these final moments
he seems painfully aware that he has lived the life of an escapist,
that he has refused to face social and political problems squarely,
that he has romanticized killing and warfare. His criticism extends
from his well-known love of the bullfight to his admiration for
Nazi generals like Rommel (T, 55).

In many ways, Hemingway's self-evaluation parallels the
*Gewissensprozeß* of Dorland in the framework of *Soldiers,* but
there it was primarily the soldier who had to face his past in the
black glass, whereas here it is the writer who takes precedence. The
drama is divided into two relatively short acts. Hochhuth must
have realized that in order to be performable, the monodrama
would have to be more economical than his previous plays. The
action takes place in a single room of Hemingway's house in
Ketchum before dawn on the morning of his death. The black
mirror of the window and the books arranged along the walls from
which Hemingway reads aloud are used as a means of expanding
the temporal and spatial dimensions, to make the room encompass
all of Hemingway's life (T, 18). There is no suspense raised as to the
eventual outcome of the action, for from the beginning Hemingway refers to what he plans to do. The audience is constantly reminded of the nearness of death as he remembers his previous attempts and his father's precedent. It is apparently only a matter of
time. Dramatic tension can therefore only be sustained by the
juxtaposition of present and past, by the struggle within the man to
place his life in perspective, to strive for honesty in these moments
of self-scrutiny. There is in fact little physical action. Hemingway
thinks that he notices the police lurking outside in the bushes at one
point and calls out to them. In the second act he even telephones
the local police to turn himself in for some imagined crime. He
occasionally tries to do something constructive, to burn some supposedly incriminating evidence, to write a check for the cleaning
lady or a letter to his sons, but he is unable to remember what he
planned to burn, and he cannot write coherently. Yet he is not
entirely helpless; he mixes himself several drinks, makes sand-
wiches, goes to get the gun, and finds the books he wishes to
consult.

In contrast to this limited physical activity, which at times seems
artificial in its abruptness, there is a tense mental action that devel-
ops throughout the monologue. The self-evaluative process begins

with a simple expression of embarassment at the *Albernheiten* (foolish remarks) to be found in even his best novels. He cites a specific example from *The Old Man and the Sea* (T, 24). Next it expresses itself by means of a contrast with the fate of another author, Herman Melville. Hemingway seems jealous of the author of *Moby Dick,* of his philosophical novels, of his depth. Although the latter's masterpieces were not recognized during his lifetime, Hemingway would trade his fate for that of Melville (T, 43). As the monodrama progresses, however, the self-examination becomes more intense, the author's insights into his failures as a writer wax more acute, and he becomes increasingly articulate. This development seems inconsistent with the portrayal of an otherwise confused and senile character. Is it realistic to assume that he could be so feeble-minded on the one hand, and yet so articulate on the other? We might surmise that Hochhuth was not entirely concerned with "Realism" in this instance, that he wanted simply to make certain observations about the role of the writer in this way.

Hemingway points out that his ego had prevented him from seriously considering the social ills of his country as a topic for his novels. He had never written a novel with a setting in the United States, but had always sought escape in exotic places like Africa or through the adventure of war, like his participation in the Spanish Civil War. Now Hochhuth pictures Hemingway as saying: "At least now look away from yourself to the suffering of one in four fellow citizens who vegetates beneath the poverty line!" (T, 51). In a sense this is a totally meaningless cry for a man about to commit suicide because he can no longer write, but it is understandable as an admonition by Hochhuth to himself and his fellow authors as well as to his listeners.

The voice of Hochhuth behind the figure of Hemingway becomes increasingly apparent as the monodrama progresses. The self-criticism becomes almost frenzied in the second act, building to a crescendo before Hemingway shoots himself, but the content reflects Hochhuth's beliefs more than Hemingway's. At one point the character states: "An author goes through his purgatory when he quotes himself . . . and admits what he did not achieve" (T, 119). This statement may in fact reflect Hochhuth's fear that despite all his efforts to speak the truth in his dramas, he had not been able to achieve all he had originally hoped.

Much of Hemingway's self-accusation in the play is based on a litany of omissions, a list of subjects he had ignored. "I never showed people on the assembly line or the farmer squeezed by mortgages and the screw manufacturer who is destroyed, not because the economy conspires against him, but because it flourishes according to its own law that the big fish eat the little ones ... in which, damn it, this country sees God's will!" (T, 77). But he is equally dissatisfied with what he has done: "The ally-enemy concept in my novels is as primitive as that of West Point academicians" (T, 72). And criticizing his war novels in particular, he says they "described wars as though they were outings," while noting that their success was due to the fact that "such books last longer than the truthful ones. The truth has very little standing in the opinion of mankind" (T, 72).[16] Occasionally during his descent to the depths of despair Hemingway achieves a moment of self-esteem, providing the necessary counterpoint. For example he takes his early novel, *To Have and Have Not,* off the shelf, a work that Hochhuth calls "the document that gives him a place in the tradition of the great social critics of literature" (T, 102). He defends himself by pointing out the fact that the character of Harry Morgan had demonstrated the powerlessness of the individual in the face of the misery of the majority of people. But Hemingway blames himself for not taking the next logical step, for failing to demonstrate "that only the community [*Gemeinschaft*] can help in this case, the new Left, for the old community of the Right had four hundred years to transform society and didn't help" (T, 103)[17] A few moments later Hemingway seems pleased with himself that he had kissed Castro's flag, but this small act of fidelity is overshadowed by the fact that he had eventually left his home in Cuba. He blames himself for a multitude of failures, for not speaking out against McCarthy in the days of the House Unamerican Activities Committee, for not recognizing the greatness of Franklin Roosevelt, but above all for escaping the real issues of poverty and war by describing the landscape of our world without asking questions about it. "Oh, I shouldn't have just described roads; I should have dealt with the question of *why* one is on the way ... or why one has no choice to go!" (T, 107–108). But such a severe evaluation of the American novelist is clearly Hochhuth's own. Hemingway's brother, for one, gave the American novelist credit for trying in his own way to improve this world: "He was absolutely dedicated to the belief that talent in the fine arts was not enough. It must be used to make the world a better place in which to live, and that included fighting for human freedom wherever it was threatened. [...] a writer should do what he could for human rights and dignity."[18] In his biography Leicester Hemingway also indicates the way in which his older brother went about doing this: "He was convinced that, for him, a better way to do something about human conditions was to show these things as clearly as he could so that men elsewhere would be incensed enough to take action. It was the beginning of a credo for him. In later years he developed it to the classic status of a moral responsibility."[19] If this assessment is correct, there is some justification in assuming that Hochhuth identified to a certain extent with his character, at least in so far as their intent was concerned.

Although *Tod eines Jägers* is a monologue of ultimate resignation, Hochhuth could not entirely forget the figure of Sisyphus in this drama. In one explanatory note he remarks of Hemingway, "the Sisyphus parable, which he didn't even know as such, had worn him out [*hat ihn leergekämpft*]" (T, 53). This suggests that, whatever his failures, Hemingway had also been engaged in that Sisyphean struggle to change society. But the battle had wasted him away, and now that his body and mind were of no use to him, now that he could no longer write, he refused to live out the comedy. Through the figure of Hemingway, Hochhuth seems to reveal his own awareness that every positive revolt which tries to change the world is made only at great personal cost. Revealing in this connection are the words which Hemingway uses to counter his critics, maintaining that they never had to fear "that insidious resignation and sadness which I had to overcome in order to write every line that said yes to life" (T, 100).[20] We can only speculate here to what extent Hochhuth actually identified with his character. But there is a suggestion throughout his *oeuvre* that he was only able to arrive at his sense of "truth through history" at a similar cost. He always vacillated between optimism and pessimism; he experienced that "fluctuation from assent to refusal" which Camus sees as characterizing the difficult task of the artist.[21] Hochhuth has certainly chosen to play the "Sisyphus game," but he seems to share that lurking fear expressed by his Hemingway figure that literature is powerless to change society ("Die Ohnmacht auch der Literatur vor der Gesellschaft" [T, 101]). Yet as long as Sisyphus has work to do — and he always will — Hochhuth seems prepared to go on.

Much of Hochhuth's importance as a dramatist during the last decade can be attributed to the kind of critical reaction he has aroused. In the case of *Tod eines Jägers,* it is too early to assess that reaction. Although the author makes it clear that he thinks that the monodrama can be performed (T, 6), no production has as yet been attempted.[22] But this monologue of resignation may also have been a way for Hochhuth to step back for a moment from his engaged position, to express his personal doubts and fears, to admonish himself about past failures, and to suggest the kinds of themes that should be dealt with in the future. At the end Hemingway makes a statement which may indeed directly reflect Hochhuth's opinion of his own work up to this point: "Then the whole world can print that what one produces is a swindle; one knows it is valuable, and this knowledge makes one unconquerable ... no, that sounds like tooting one's own horn, it makes one composed —" (T, 120). It is the attainment of this composure (*Gelassenheit*) that finally enables Hemingway to commit suicide, for at this point he is reconciled with his life and therefore with death. The achievement of such composure for Hochhuth suggests, instead, preparedness for struggles yet to come.

CHAPTER 8

# *Conclusion*

T HERE are always inherent difficulties in evaluating a living
author — for instance, the lack of distance, the problem of an
incomplete *oeuvre*. In Hochhuth's case these factors are further
complicated by the unusual nature of his career and the controversial nature of his dramas. Yet after a decade of writing, in which he
has produced not only six major dramas, but numerous essays,
poetry, and narrative prose, an evaluation of his contribution to
German and world literature is legitimate, although it must remain
provisional. I have chosen to consider Hochhuth primarily as a
dramatist and secondly as an essayist, since he has concentrated his
literary efforts in these two genres. His international reputation,
however, rests exclusively on his work as a playwright.

Hochhuth's importance can be measured in part by the level of
controversy that has surrounded his plays. Many critics have dismissed his *oeuvre* out of hand because of what they see as his out-
moded view of the world and his use of traditional dramatic conventions. Still others have rejected his dramas at the outset because
they believe that political intent has no place in art. But politics and
art are not mutually exclusive; even polemics do not necessarily
interfere with the overall aesthetic effect. The refusal to take Hochhuth seriously on either artistic or political grounds is not a fruitful
approach. Yet the fact that his *oeuvre* has been put into question in
both these respects has ironically contributed to his importance, by
placing him at the center of an ongoing debate as to what *is* possible
in drama in our contemporary world. In this monograph I have
critically analyzed Hochhuth's dramas without rejecting *a priori*
either his concept of the role of the dramatist or his dramaturgy.

In his introduction to *The Deputy,* Erwin Piscator expressed the
following hope for the reception of the play: "I hope that the value
of such a work lies not only in the artistic, the formal, the aesthetic

sphere, but first and last in its words and with its reach into life; I hope this play will be a force *for change.*"[1] Such a hope might have been raised by the author himself for all his subsequent plays, for they were written in exactly the same spirit. Hochhuth expected his plays to generate discussion; even at his most pessimistic he conceived of the theater as a moral institution and hoped to bring about change. But it is practically impossible to measure this kind of effect. The reactions evidenced by audiences at performances of plays or the citing of theater statistics (box office success) are inadequate indicators. They cannot show to what extent people reflect on the issues presented or to what extent individuals or institutions are eventually affected. In Hochhuth's case, we must also consider the fact that the object of discussion was often quite drastically altered by a director, and that his dramas have generated as much discussion among a reading public which has never witnessed a performance of the plays.

Many critics, and even writers like Max Frisch, have suggested that playwrights like Hochhuth have overestimated the role which the theater can play in influencing the world. Despite his commitment to the theater as a moral institution, Hochhuth does share some of this skepticism. He has always feared that his dramas were an inadequate vehicle for bringing about change. It is undoubtedly for this reason that he has expressed his political and philosophical positions in essays that often accompanied or defended the plays. He has also expressed an awareness that the effectiveness of a drama will depend entirely on whether it reaches an appropriate audience. "The writer is powerless by himself; not what he writes, but whom he is able to reach, decides whether he is heard or not" (K, 69).[2] The validity of this statement is shown by the story behind *The Deputy.* If Erwin Piscator and Ledig-Rowohlt had not had the courage to bring it to the stage and to publish it, it could never have received the response it did. Hochhuth did succeed, however, in unleashing, in this instance, the kind of discussion among historians, philosophers, literary critics, churchmen, and laymen that he desired. His *Soldiers* also succeeded on this level. Ironically, both plays were performed more often outside Germany, yet they were instrumental in shaping the future of German drama in the 1960s and 1970s.

It was inconceivable that Hochhuth could continue to evoke this same kind of world response with his next play. Despite the American setting and the importance of the theme of revolution, *Guerillas* was directed primarily to a German audience. But even there it failed to have the same resonance, primarily because it was artistically less successful. Here polemics did interfere with poetics. The aesthetically more effective works had the more far-reaching political impact. With *Die Hebamme* Hochhuth once again directed his attention to a specifically middle class German audience. And the Kassel production indicated that in the hands of an imaginative director this comedy could have an impact — at least within Germany — that caused people to reflect on the issues raised and aroused the ire of local politicians who felt themselves under attack.

There can be no doubt that the first two tragedies and the first comedy had the kind of initial impact which the author had sought. On this level they were successful. Too often critics dismiss such successes as too short-lived to be important. A case in point: in comparing Ionesco to the German documentary dramatists, Allan Lewis has stated: "The German plays are now safely ensconced in the archives. *Waiting for Godot* will outlive *The Deputy*. It is doubtful in any case to what extent a play can influence events."[3] Hochhuth would certainly argue that his plays do not try to influence events but people, and in turn institutions, through a portrayal of the conflict of ideas. Furthermore, it is useless to make predictions as to which play will "outlive" another, as though the ability to become a "classic" at some later date could provide the key to its significance for the present. In the case of Hochhuth's first two plays, the intensity of the initial reception was indeed the important thing; the dramas were intended to have a particular effect in the present and they clearly achieved this result. We cannot really speculate as to whether these plays will survive in the sense intended by Lewis. Other critics have been willing to make equally dire predictions to the contrary. In speaking of *The Deputy,* for example, Egon Schwarz has predicted: "[it is] a significant drama which will continue to provide a glimpse into the most horrible abyss in our culture, long after anyone but a few church historians will remember who Pius XII was."[4]

By comparing Ionesco's drama to Hochhuth's, Lewis has suggested another problem that has characterized so much of Hochhuth criticism — people's unwillingness to accept his traditional dramaturgy. In *The Theatre of the Absurd,* Martin Esslin has argued eloquently that the plays written in this new convention could not be fairly judged by the standards and criteria of another, quite different, convention.[5] The same argument must now be made in reverse on behalf of Hochhuth. In the early 1960s, when the Absurd convention had become acceptable, an intolerance toward the more traditional dramatic mode could be registered. This was responsible for the "So-kann-man-doch-kein-Drama-schreiben" ("you-can't-write-drama-that-way") response that so often greeted Hochhuth's plays. But it should be stressed once more that Hochhuth's dramaturgy, with its reliance on individualized personages, a realistic treatment of place and time, and a conflict of ideas, is entirely consistent with the author's world view and should be judged in terms of its own convention, not by comparing it with a different one.

In his statement of hope for the reception of *The Deputy,* Piscator had emphasized the political aspect. But he did not ignore aesthetics entirely. And there is nothing in Hochhuth's essays or dramas to suggest that he wanted his *oeuvre* to be judged only by its content. In fact, he has continually stressed that his plays are works of art — not reportage. And it is the aesthetic aspect which is the primary concern of the literary critic. For this reason, I have not stressed the historical validity of Hochhuth's arguments in this monograph. Despite a certain subjectivity inherent in all literary criticism, there do seem to be some objective standards which can be used to measure Hochhuth's success or failure in this area, as, for example: (1) suggestive power, (2) originality, (3) psychological truth, (4) depth and universality of theme, (5) degree of skill in translating ideas to the stage, (6) intensity and coherence of the imaginative whole, (7) the profoundly experienced emotion from which the work springs.[6]

Hochhuth's greatest strength as a writer has been the extent to which he has fulfilled the last of these criteria. All his works, both dramatic and essayistic, are imbued with a profound sense of emotion, springing from his true concern for the situation of man and his conviction that the writer must do the little he can to change that condition. We cannot doubt the sincerity of Hochhuth's convictions — even when they seem naive — because of the consistency with which he has expressed them in his essays and dramas. The skill with which he has been able to give his views dramatic form has been of varying quality. Hochhuth has shown signs of great originality, in part due to his uncanny sense of topicality. This was particularly true of his first two plays; their importance as dramas is directly linked to the importance of the material. *Lysistrate und die Nato* is the least original of his plays, and for this as well as for other more compelling reasons, it is the weakest. Hochhuth's first two dramas also have strong suggestive power. They are at once realistic and symbolic; they suggest a truth that goes beyond the factual truth of history. Both have a depth and universality of theme, despite the specific references to the past and present, which raise them above the level of "pure documentation." *The Deputy* raises ultimate questions of faith, guilt, and responsibility, especially in Act V, which is necessary to the logic of the play, whatever its deficiencies as drama. *Tod eines Jägers* also asks important questions as to the meaning and purpose of our lives, not only of the author who is its main character, but of all men. Although the questions of revolution, poverty, and war raised in *Guerillas, Die Hebamme,* and *Lysistrate,* respectively, are equally universal, none of these plays was able to achieve the same level of transcendence as the first two. A return to that level in *Tod eines Jägers* suggests that Hochhuth has now ·gone through a difficult apprenticeship — delayed perhaps by his first sensational successes — an experience from which his future works will hopefully benefit.

Nearly all of Hochhuth's dramas can be described as "intense"; they rarely leave the reader or viewer indifferent. It is a quality that is dictated by the playwright's driving sense of moral outrage. But not all the plays are equally coherent as works of art. We have already pointed out specific weaknesses when discussing individual dramas, but in making an overall evaluation, we can safely say that *The Deputy* and *Soldiers* were able to make up by their intensity and the importance of their themes for whatever they lacked in coherence of plot, characterization, or language. The same cannot be said of the other plays, although *Die Hebamme* and *Tod eines Jägers* are of a much higher calibre as imaginative works of art than either *Guerillas* or *Lysistrate und die Nato.* Perhaps Hochhuth himself recognized the weakness of the latter two plays because in each case they signaled a change to a different mode — comedy and monodrama. If accepted as a *Volksstück, Die Hebamme* has some merit; it is certainly a better comedy than *Lysistrate.* But what is particularly disturbing about the latter is the extent to which a puerile eroticism — already apparent in scenes between the doctor and Helga in *The Deputy* — totally masks the theme of war. *Tod eines Jägers* presents a welcome return to more serious subjects, portrayed in a way that can be taken seriously.

Hochhuth has had only mixed success in translating his ideas to the stage. This is due in part to the fact that his dramas are too long to be performed integrally. Yet the author intended his plays for the stage. His lack of self-control in this respect — however problematic for directors — is part of his distinctive literary style, adding to the total impact of the dramas when read. In fact, an evaluation of his plays as performed might differ significantly from an evaluation of the texts.[7] The much shorter length of *Tod eines Jägers* would indicate that Hochhuth may be moving away from his laborious narrative style. Yet even with this play there is some question about its performability, because it is a monodrama. Here the author has also returned to a more poetic idiom — free verse — which he first employed in *The Deputy* as a way of avoiding Naturalism on the one hand, and a classical poetic language on the other. His experimentation with this kind of heightened language — neither poetry nor prose — while not always successful in practice, has been one of his important contributions to contemporary German drama.

Hochhuth has also been important in Germany as a theoretician. Although he has been given credit for directing the attention of the world to German drama in the early 1960s, little has been said of his efforts to draw the attention of German dramatists and critics to the problem of Realism. This accomplishment has often been overlooked on the international scene because of the furor over individual plays. Hochhuth was ridiculed at first for his attempt to reinstate the tragic hero, but in so doing he stimulated discussion of how the epic and the tragic could be combined. Rainer Taëni pointed this out in his interesting analysis of *The Deputy,* reaching the conclusion that polemics and tragedy are not necessarily mutually exclusive.[8]

It is difficult to assess just how much influence Hochhuth's concept of Realism has exerted on other dramatists. Critics have usually interpreted his role as that of forerunner in the area of documentary drama. But his own rejection of this term, as well as his turn to more fictive creations, indicates that this feature of his dramatic practice — while important for German drama in the 1960s — has been overemphasized at the expense of his appreciation of the tragic or the Absurd as part of a theater of Realism.

In a recent appraisal of German drama between 1965 and 1975, Günter Rühle has noted a gradual return to a theater of Realism, especially after 1970. Ödön von Horváth, not Brecht, became the model for younger writers. Some dramatists even looked to Ibsen's well-made plays, in which figures are treated as individuals yet mirror their times. Nowhere does Rühle mention Hochhuth in this development, yet his description of what playwrights were finding in the "rediscovered" plays of the 1920s could have been a description of Hochhuth's stated goals: "The persons [in these rediscovered plays] are always suffering, demanding struggling human beings, even in situations where their ineffectiveness [*Ohnmacht*] is readily apparent. That means that [the authors of the 1920s] have always treated life as life, perceived it as a conflict. Thus they also preserved drama as drama, even in the plays about current affairs [*Zeitstück*]."[9]

It seems ironic that Hochhuth is practically a forgotten figure in recent German criticism, for it was he who first demonstrated, in *The Deputy,* just such a struggling individual hero. And it has been Hochhuth who has largely championed the conflict-oriented drama over the last decade in Germany. Despite all the changes in his dramaturgy, he has never wavered in his basic commitment to the individual human being as a dramatic personage or to the drama as a conflict situation. Even his most recent drama, *Tod eines Jägers,* continues this pattern, for it dramatizes the internal conflict of a real individual. Hochhuth's contribution to this new wave of Realism in German drama since 1970 should not be underestimated.

In both his essays and dramas over the last thirteen years Hochhuth has discussed the role of the theater in politics, the possibilities for tragedy and comedy in contemporary drama, the role of language as a means of rising to the level of ideas from the purely documentary level, and, most importantly, the role of the writer as citizen. His contribution to these discussions may, in the long run, be more significant for German and world literature than any one of his dramas. It is revealing that the role of the writer as citizen reasserted itself as a theme in *Tod eines Jägers.* After repeatedly rolling his stone to the top of the hill, only to see it tumble down again, Hochhuth's view of his role has remained unchanged: The artist must continue to play the Sisyphus game; he must continue to articulate the bad conscience of his country and the world, because those in positions of power hesitate to do so. Although we cannot predict where Hochhuth will go from here, we can safely assume that he will continue to raise his voice in this effort, for "Sisyphus wird nie arbeitslos" ("Sisyphus will never be out of work" [H, 420]).

# Notes and References

## Chapter One

1. Dietrich Strothmann, "Das schlechte Gewissen der Nation: Rolf Hochhuth benutzt das Theater als politische Anstalt," *Die Zeit,* 20 October 1967, p. 2.

2. Judy Stone, "Interview with Rolf Hochhuth," in Eric Bentley, ed., *The Storm over The Deputy* (New York, 1964), pp. 42–47 (hereafter cited as *Storm*).

3. *Ibid.,* p. 46.

4. *Ibid.,* p. 47.

5. The early prose in *Die Hebamme* (Reinbek, 1971) includes the short story "Resignation oder die Geschichte einer Ehe" (1959) and *Die Berliner Antigone* (1961). The poetry is not dated.

6. Stone, p. 48.

7. Friedrich Dürrenmatt, *Problems of the Theatre: An Essay,* trans. Gerhard Nellhaus (New York, 1958), p. 29. For the original see Friedrich Dürrenmatt, *Theaterprobleme* (Zürich, 1955), p. 43.

8. Martin Esslin, "A Playwright who drops political Blockbusters," *New York Times Magazine,* 19 November 1967, p. 160.

9. Although not a dictionary entry, the use of the world "personalization" here and elsewhere is an attempt on the author's part to translate the German term *Personalisierung* used by both Hochhuth and his critics. The term is not intended to replace *Personifizierung* (personification), but indicates an attitude that affirms the worth of the individual human being and his ability to act and assume responsibility for his actions. As Fritz J. Raddatz indicates in his introduction to *Krieg und Klassenkrieg* (Reinbek, 1971): "Hochhuth argumentiert *ad personam*" (K, 9).

10. Esslin, pp. 160–62.

11. Friedrich Schiller, "Über die tragische Kunst," in *Sämtliche Werke* (Munich, 1960), V, 390.

12. Patricia Marx, "Interview with Rolf Hochhuth," in *Storm,* pp. 56–57.

13. Peter Weiss, "Das Material und die Modelle," *Dramen* (Frankfurt am Main, 1968), II, 465–67.

14. Marx, pp. 55–56. See also Rolf Hochhuth, "Er sah das Tragische nicht: Ein Brief über Bertolt Brecht," *Theater heute,* February 1967, p. 8.

15. Esslin, pp. 160–62.

16. Friedrich Schiller, "Was kann eine gute stehende Schaubühne eigentlich wirken oder Die Schaubühne als moralische Anstalt betrachtet," in *Sämtliche Werke,* V, 818–31.

17. Stone, p. 43.

18. *Ibid.,* p. 58.

19. Quoted by Ulrich Weisstein in *Max Frisch* (New York, 1967), p. 123. The original source of this quotation is cited by Weisstein as *Jahrbuch der deutschen Akademie für Sprache und Dichtung* (Heidelberg, 1958), p. 95.

## Chapter Two

1. Marx, pp. 54–55. Hochhuth must be referring here to Leon Poliakov, *Das Dritte Reich und die Juden* (Berlin, 1955).

2. *Ibid.,* p. 55.

3. *Ibid.,* p. 54. For Holthusen's reactions to *The Deputy* see his letter to Hochhuth in *Summa iniuria oder Durfte der Papst schweigen?,* ed. Fritz J. Raddatz (Reinbek, 1963), pp. 22–24.

4. Siegfried Melchinger, *Hochhuth,* Friedrichs Dramatiker des Welttheaters 44 (Velber bei Hannover, 1967), pp. 8–9.

5. See Hannah Arendt, *Eichmann in Jerusalem* (New York, 1963); and Bernd Naumann, *Auschwitz: A report on the proceedings against Robert Karl Ludwig Mulka and others before the court at Frankfurt,* trans. Jean Steinberg (New York, 1966). See also Peter Weiss, *Die Ermittlung,* in *Dramen,* II, 7–199.

6. Erwin Piscator, *Das Politische Theater,* in *Schriften I* (Berlin Ost, 1968).

7. Erwin Piscator, "Introduction to *The Deputy,*" trans. Clara Mayer, in *Storm,* p. 13. See also St, 7–11; and Dr, 7–10, for original.

8. *Ibid.,* p. 15.

9. The emphasis on the "truth" of Hochhuth's historical thesis is reflected in the titles of the books that appeared on the subject, most of them within a year of the Berlin premiere: Walter Adolph, *Verfälschte Geschichte* (Berlin, 1963); Rosario F. Esposito, *Processo al vicario* (Turin, 1964); Josef M. Görgen, *Pius XII, Katholische Kirche und Hochhuths 'Stellvertreter'* (Buxheim, 1964); Jenö Levai, *Geheime Reichssache — Papst Pius XII hat nicht geschwiegen* (Cologne, 1966); Jacques Nobecourt, *"Le Vicaire" et l'histoire* (Paris, 1964).

10. For an account of this production see Melchinger, p. 105.

11. For further discussion of this problem see Rainer Taëni, "'Der Stellvertreter': Episches Theater oder christliche Tragödie?" *Seminar,* II, no. 1 (Spring 1966), 29–30.

12. John Simon, "*The Deputy* and its Metamorphoses," in *Storm,* p. 116.

13. Susan Sontag, "Reflections on *The Deputy,*" in *Storm,* p. 121.

14. *Ibid.,* pp. 117-18.

15. *Ibid.,* p. 120.

16. Manfred Durzak, *Dürrenmatt, Frisch, Weiss: Deutsches Drama der Gegenwart zwischen Kritik und Utopie* (Stuttgart, 1972), p. 28.

17. Piscator, "Introduction to *The Deputy,*" pp. 11-12.

18. "Gott ist kalt, die Hände werden mir steif, wenn ich sie falte./ Und die Götter der Alten sind tot wie ihre Sagen und wie/ das antike Geröll im Museum des Vatikans, im/ Beinhaus der Kunst" (St, 181).

19. "...das ist nicht einmal vorstellbar, geschweige denn atmosphärisch anzudeuten" (St, 182).

20. For reviews of this production see *Storm,* pp. 16-34.

21. Rolf C. Zimmermann, "Drama or Pamphlet: Hochhuth's *The Deputy* and the Tradition of Polemical Literature," trans. Abe Farbstein, in *Storm,* p. 133. This article also appeared in the collection *Der Streit um Hochhuths 'Stellvertreter'* (Basle, 1963).

22. *Ibid.,* pp. 137-38.

23. *Ibid.,* p. 147.

24. For further information about individual productions see Melchinger, pp. 104-108.

25. Melchinger, p. 12.

26. *Ibid.,* p. 13. See also "A German J'accuse," *Time,* 6 March 1964, p. 42.

27. See "Character Assassination," in *Storm,* pp. 39-41, editorial reprinted from *America,* 7 March 1964.

28. Heinz von Cramer, "Nicht Hochhuth ist der Demagoge," in *Summa iniuria,* pp. 48-50.

29. Pater Robert Leiber SJ, "Der Papst und die Verfolgung der Juden," in *Summa iniuria,* pp. 101-107. A more detailed study of Pius XII by Pater Leiber had been published in *Stimmen der Zeit,* November 1958. For an English translation by Salvator Attanasio of the latter article see *Storm,* pp. 173-95.

30. G. B. Cardinal Montini, "Pius XII and the Jews," in *Storm,* p. 67 (originally appeared in *The Tablet,* June 1963).

31. *Ibid.,* p. 68.

32. Rolf Hochhuth, "Reply to Cardinal Montini," trans. William Duell, Jr., in *Storm,* pp. 69-71.

33. Friedrich Heer, "The Need for Confession," in *Storm,* p. 173 (originally appeared in *Commonweal*).

34. "A Statement by Francis Cardinal Spellman," in *Storm,* pp. 37-38.

35. Fritz J. Raddatz, "Vorbemerkung," *Summa iniuria,* p. 8.

36. See *Storm,* pp. 237-54.

37. For the Albert Schweitzer letter see Rolf Hochhuth, *The Deputy,* trans. Richard and Clara Winston (New York, 1964), p. 7. For Karl Jaspers' reactions see Melchinger, p. 13, and *Storm,* pp. 99–102.

38. Golo Mann, "The Real Accomplishment," trans. William Duell Jr., in *Storm,* p. 219.

39. *Ibid.,* p. 218.

40. For the complete text of the Mann essay in German see Dr, 284–85.

41. Walter Muschg, "Hochhuth and Lessing," in *Dramen,* pp. 285–87. This article first appeared in the program of the Frankfurt production. It was included in the rororo-theater 997/998 edition of *Der Stellvertreter* (Reinbek, 1967), and in *Jahresband der Deutschen Dramaturgischen Gesellschaft* (1964).

42. "Sie zeigen, wie tief verschüttet in Deutschland die Tradition der freiheitlichen, kämpferischen Dichtung ist, die von der Aufklärung über das Junge Deutschland bis zum Expressionismus führt" (Dr, 285).

43. See *Summa iniuria,* pp. 124–40. Hochhuth republished this response to Alff in the collection of essays, *Krieg und Klassenkrieg* (K, 181–91), thus revealing the importance he attributed to it.

44. "Aus vorwiegend richtigen Quellen zeichnet Hochhuth ein falsches Bild, weil das wirkliche Geschichtsbild des Europa der Jahre 1942 bis 1944 ihm nicht gegenwärtig ist.... Die unklaren Quellen, aus denen er schöpft, sind nicht die der Dokumente, sondern die des eigenen falschen Bewußtseins." *Summa iniuria,* p. 132.

## Chapter Three

1. Strothmann, p. 2. Also *The File on "Soldiers": Historical Notes on Rolf Hochhuth's Play,* ed. Kathleen Tynan ([England] n.d., n.p.), p. 6.

2. "Interview mit Rolf Hochhuth," *Die Zeit,* 6 October 1967, p. 19. See also Hans Mayer, "Jedermann und Churchill," *Die Zeit,* 13 October 1967, p. 16. The title of R. M. Lenz' "comedy" was *Die Soldaten,* and like Hochhuth, who dropped the definite article, he hoped to influence his contemporaries not only with the drama but with a pamphlet that accompanied the play, arguing against the forced bachelorhood of soldiers which had led to the abuse of so many young ladies in garrison towns.

3. *The File on "Soldiers",* pp. 23–24. See also "Interview," *Die Zeit,* p. 19.

4. *The File on "Soldiers",* pp. 5–6. See also, *Krieg und Klassenkrieg,* p. 110. For further information see David Irving, *The Destruction of Dresden* (London, 1963) or *Der Untergang Dresdens* (Gütersloh, 1964).

5. "Wir Deutschen zuerst bleiben dieser Jahrhundertfigur für immer verpflichtet, weil sie — neben den russischen Soldaten — wohl das höchste Verdienst hat an der Befreiung Europas von dem durch uns heraufbeschworenen Hitler. Aber der böse Geist von Dresden, die entsetzlichen Verir-

rungen Churchills, die unzähligen Zivilisten den Tod brachten, ohne beizutragen zum Sieg der Alliierten, sie mögen dann mit ihm ins Grab sinken" (K, 129). At the time Hochhuth wrote this letter Churchill lay on his deathbed.

6. "Allein von Ihrer persönlichen Initiative, verehrter Herr Bundespräsident, hängt jetzt ab, ob in der Welt die augenblicklich unbegrenzte Gewalt eingeschränkt wird, die sich seit den Bombardements im Zweiten Weltkrieg die Luftstrategen aller Armeen über die Frauen und Kinder und Alten fremder und eigener Länder angemaßt haben" (K, 128).

7. The title accompanying the letter in this volume reiterates the theme, "Vom Soldaten zum Berufsverbrecher" ("From Soldier to Professional Criminal"), but the introductory remarks reveal that the situation had not changed between 1964 and 1971 (K, 106–107).

8. *The File on "Soldiers"*, p. 3.

9. Esslin, p. 152. An interesting sidelight on this problem is revealed in the imaginary conversation between Hochhuth and his publisher, Ledig-Rowohlt, in "L'Impromptu de Madame Tussaud" (H, 54–55 and 58–59).

10. *The File on "Soldiers"*, p. 6.

11. *Ibid.*, p. 26. See also David Irving, *Accident: The Death of General Sikorski* (London, 1967) or *Moskaus Staatsräson? Sikorski und Churchill — eine tragische Allianz* (Munich, 1969).

12. "...niemals hat Piscator gemeint, daß Dokumentation schon Kunst sei. Daß ungefilterter historischer Schutt, schaufelt man ihn nur auf die Bühne, schon zur Szene würde oder die Kommandos der Aktivisten zur Sprache. Piscator meinte nichts anderes als Goethe, wenn der sagte, er habe die Wirklichkeit stets für genialer gehalten als sein Genie. Das *Studium* der Wirklichkeit, nicht ihre 'Einblendung', wie man momentan sagt, nicht ihre Abschrift war für Piscator eine Voraussetzung — eine! — seiner politischen Kunst" (H, 458).

13. Esslin, pp. 157–58.

14. Quoted in *Ibid.*, p. 160.

15. The German editions are clearly designated with the word "Tragödie," (So, title page; and Dr, 289). This designation was carried over in the British edition (London, 1968) but not in the American edition (New York, 1968), even though the translation in both cases was by Robert David MacDonald.

16. *The File on "Soldiers"*, p. 5. See also "Interview," *Die Zeit*, p. 19.

17. By way of comparison, in *Dramen, Der Stellvertreter* runs 280 pages, *Soldaten* only 185 pages. But in the latter all historical data were included in the text or in stage notes — there are no separate "Historical Sidelights."

18. *The File on "Soldiers"*, pp. 5–6. See also "Interview," *Die Zeit*, p. 19.

19. Hochhuth made the same point when he let the wax figure of Chur-

chill, which appears in "L'Impromptu de Madame Tussaud," state: "und wenn mich erst meine Auseinandersetzung mit Sikorski tragödienreif gemacht hat — warum nicht! Lebendig will man sein, nach dem Tode, nicht 'unschuldig'" (H, 68).

20. The title *Everyman* was taken from the medieval play (1529) of the same name, and *The Little London Theater of the World* was derived from Calderón's *El Gran Teatro del Mundo* (S, 13–14). But Hochhuth may also have had in mind Hugo von Hofmannsthal, who wrote a modern *Jedermann* and a play entitled *Salzburger Großes Welttheater.*

21. Stanley Kaufmann, "Rolf Hochhuth's *Soldaten* in New York," *Die Zeit,* 24 May 1968, p. 17. See also Christopher Driver, "London — ohne Zensur," *Die Zeit,* 20 December 1968, p. 20.

22. The photograph was also included in the British edition, p. 24, but not in the American edition published by Grove Press.

23. Reinhard Baumgart, "Unmenschlichkeit beschrieben," in *Publik: Materialien zur Zeit,* Publication of Freie Volksbühne (Berlin), no. 1 (1967), 12–16.

24. The English translation unfortunately does not use the word cabaret. "It should be clear that the music-hall atmosphere here is purely formal. The facts, on the other hand, are incredible but true, and accessible in the *Frankfurter Allgemeine* of January 13, 1967, or the *Basler Nachrichten* of February 18, 1967" (S, 49).

25. Ironically, the frame itself was eventually cut in this production, and thus the significance of this change in casting was lost.

26. Peter Weiss, *Diskurs über die Vorgeschichte und den Verlauf des lang andauernden Befreiungskrieges in Viet Nam als Beispiel für die Notwendigkeit des bewaffneten Kampfes der Unterdrückten gegen ihre Unterdrücker sowie über die Versuche der Vereinigten Staaten von Amerika die Grundlagen der Revolution zu vernichten,* in *Dramen,* II, 267–456.

27. Rolf Hochhuth, "Dieser Pole starb gelegen," *Der Spiegel,* 2 October 1967, pp. 133–34, 136–42; and Rolf Hochhuth, "Noch Fünfzig Jahre Schweigen," *Der Spiegel,* 9 October 1967, pp. 164, 166–67, 169–72, 174. Excerpts from the second act of the play were also published under the words attributed to Lord Cherwell, "Jetzt aber runter mit dem Polacken," *Der Spiegel,* 9 October 1967, pp. 177–78, 180, 182, 185–88, 190–91.

28. Hochhuth, "Dieser Pole starb gelegen," p. 133. Even the title is a literary reminiscence: Schiller, *Maria Stuart* (Act IV, Scene 6) — Burleigh: "Graf, dieser Mortimer starb euch sehr gelegen." — in *Sämtliche Werke,* II, 649.

29. Ludwig Marcuse, "Hochhuth und seine Verächter," in *Dramen,* pp. 475–81). See also Strothmann, p. 2.

30. A typical example: Heinz Ritter, "Hochhuth kam vor dem Fall," *Der Abend,* 10 October 1967, p. 10. The subtitles for this article read "Die 'Premiere des Jahres' endete mit einer Niederlage," and "Ein großes

Thema wurde verzettelt." For further reviews see: Ruth Römstedt, "Hochhuths Flirt mit der Wahrheit," *Berliner Leben,* November 1967, pp. 9–10; Felix Henseleit, "*Soldaten* — und was die Kritik dazu meint: Jahrhundertgestalt im Zwielicht," *Berliner Leben,* November 1967, p. 12; Günther Rühle, "Revision für Hochhuth," *Theater heute,* November 1967, p. 3; Henning Rischbieter, "Realität, Poesie, Politik: Monströs mißlungen, 'Soldaten' von Hochhuth," *Theater heute,* November 1967, pp. 16–17.

31. This analysis is based on my personal observations during a later performance of this production, although other critics noted this problem.

32. See Melchinger, p. 109; Ritter, p. 10; Mayer, p. 16.

33. Mayer, p. 16. Walter Muschg made a similar argument with regard to *The Deputy* in "Hochhuth und Lessing" (Dr, 285–87).

34. "Wenn Lessing schrieb, der Dichter sei der Herr der Geschichte — ich habe mich stets als ihr Knecht gefühlt. Und das hat seinen Preis, den selbst Große bar zahlen mußten: je sklavischer man den Tatsachen der Historie Mitspracherecht auch im Kunstwerk einräumt, je verdrossener muß man mit Schiller seufzen: 'Meine Geschichte hat viel Dichterkraft in mir verdorben'" (K, 193).

35. Peter Weiss, "Das Material und die Modelle," pp. 464–72. See also Weiss' *Gesang vom Lusitanischen Popanz,* in *Dramen,* II, 202–65. For comments on the way in which both Weiss and Hochhuth expected language to heighten reality in the work of art see Melchinger, pp. 45–46. See also Heinar Kipphardt, "Wahrheit wichtiger als Wirkung," in *Deutsche Dramaturgie der Sechziger Jahre,* ed. Helmut Kreuzer (Tübingen, 1974), pp. 45–46.

36. Mayer, p. 16.

37. Clive Barnes, "Die englischsprachige Premiere," in *Dramen,* pp. 477–79. Original, "The English language premiere," *New York Times,* 3 March 1968, p. 88.

38. Jack Kroll, "Das Herz der Geschichte," in *Dramen,* pp. 479–81. Original, "The heart of the matter," *Newsweek,* 11 March 1968, p. 105.

39. Kauffmann, p. 17.

40. Driver, p. 20.

41. Ludwig Marcuse, "Hochhuth und seine Verächter," in *Dramen,* p. 476. This article first appeared in *Theater heute,* November 1967, p. 2.

42. See *Krieg und Klassenkrieg,* p. 216; and the book review by Hochhuth, "Zum Ruhme Sir Winstons," *Die Zeit,* 20 December 1968, pp. 27–29.

43. Fritz Rumler, "Poetische Rache für das deutsche Volk?" *Der Spiegel,* 20 January 1969, pp. 118–19. See also the book review of Carlos Thompson's *The Assassination of Winston Churchill* (Gerrards Cross, 1969) by Karl-Heinz Wocker, "Widerliche Wahrheitsfindung," *Die Zeit,* 21 October 1969, p. 16.

44. Quoted in Strothmann, p. 2.

45. This introduction, written in October 1968, was published first in the British edition and later in translation in *Dramen,* p. 291. It was not used in the American edition of the play.

## *Chapter Four*

1. For studies of Peter Weiss' development as an engaged author see: Otto F. Best, *Peter Weiss: Vom existentialistischen Drama zum Marxistischen Welttheater, eine kritische Bilanz* (Berne, 1971); Reinhard Meier, *Peter Weiss: Von der Exilsituation zum politischen Engagement,* Diss. Zurich, 1971 (Zurich: Juris, 1971); Margaret E. Ward, *Peter Weiss, Rolf Hochhuth, Armand Gatti: The Interaction between Intent, Content and Form in Contemporary Political Drama* (Dissertation Indiana University, 1973), pp. 1–65.

2. Rolf Hochhuth, "Der Klassenkampf ist nicht zu Ende," *Der Spiegel,* 26 May 1965, pp. 28–44.

3. Peter Weiss, "Enzensbergers Illusionen," *Kursbuch,* 6 (July 1966), 165–70; "Che Guevara!" *Kursbuch,* 11 (1968), 1–6; *Vietnam!,* Voltaire Flugschrift, 1 (Berlin, 1966).

4. A typical example of Hochhuth's polemical style is the following: "In Cologne, where the city government is known to have a social conscience, there is nevertheless every year an absolute increase of one thousand homeless [*Obdachlosen*]. A city the size of Mannheim could be completely occupied by the poor of the ghettos — all this in a country whose chancellor — thanks to his government busyness [*Geschäftigkeit*] — never meets any of the proletarians" (K, 23).

5. *Plädoyer für eine neue Regierung: 25 deutsche Autoren zum Bundestagswahlkampf* (Reinbek, 1965) appeared only shortly after the article in *Der Spiegel.* See "Die Diskussion des Aufrufs zum Klassenkampf," in *Krieg und Klassenkrieg,* pp. 49–86. Ludwig Erhard was then chancellor of the Federal Republic and head of the Christian Democratic Union (CDU). Franz Josef Strauß was head of the sister Bavarian party (CSU). Willy Brandt was leader of the Socialist party (SPD). Axel Springer was head of the powerful publication conglomerate, Springer Verlag; and Rudolf Augstein was the editor of *Der Spiegel.*

6. Karl-Heinz Janßen, "Der Pessimist im Dorfkrug: Rolf Hochhuth und Berlins Studenten: durch Welten getrennt," *Die Zeit,* 22 December 1967, p. 4.

7. A demonstration took place in Frankfurt on this date. The passage of the emergency laws — enabling acts similar to those that had helped Hitler in his rise to power — was an issue which united the leftist students in the late 1960s. Both moderate and radical authors joined with them in opposition to these laws, but they were eventually passed by the West German parliament (*Bundestag*) in the summer of 1968.

8. Hochhuth quoted here from the philosopher Karl Jaspers, who had become his personal friend after the publication of *The Deputy.* Jaspers' professorship at the University of Basle may have had something to do with Hochhuth's choice of that city as a residence (see Melchinger, p. 28).

9. Hochhuth's pun refers here to the novel by Hermann Hesse, *Das Glasperlenspiel (The Glass Bead Game).*

10. Hochhuth quotes here from the British author Edward Luttwak, but gives no specific source for the quotation. Hochhuth felt so indebted to this historian that he dedicated the essay to him (K, 217). For further background on Luttwak see *Krieg und Klassenkrieg,* pp. 224–26.

11. The translation of this passage is made difficult by the play on the different uses of the word *"Masse"* in German. In the original it reads: "Humanität ist aber immer nur dort, wo der Mensch noch oder wieder als einzelner betrachtet wird, nicht als Angehöriger einer Gruppe. Zur Masse gehört man selber, oder die Masse gibt es nicht. Es gibt eine Masse Geld, aber keine Menschen-Masse und keine Massen-Menschen" (K, 44).

12. Theodor W. Adorno, "Offener Brief an Rolf Hochhuth," *Theater heute,* July 1967, p. 1.

13. *Ibid.,* p. 2.

14. *Ibid.*

15. Although Hochhuth did not respond in the August issue, he had been interviewed in February of that year; see "Gespräch mit Siegfried Melchinger," *Theater heute,* February 1967, pp. 6–8.

16. Fritz J. Raddatz, "Die Verantwortung des Intellektuellen: Zum Impetus der Arbeiten Rolf Hochhuths," in *Krieg und Klassenkrieg,* p. 9.

17. *Ibid.,* p. 14.

18. Walter Hinck, "Von der Parabel zum Straßentheater: Notizen zum Drama der Gegenwart," in *Poesie und Politik: Zur Situation der Literatur in Deutschland,* ed. Wolfgang Kuttenkeuler (Stuttgart, 1973), p. 71. Here Hinck suggests "die Überzeugung von der Durchschaubarkeit der Welt," as one of the three prerequisites for Brecht's political theater.

## Chapter Five

1. Hochhuth traveled to the United States a the time of the openings of both *The Deputy* and *Soldiers* on Broadway. He even took part on May 1, 1968, according to one report, in anti-Vietnam War demonstrations there. See Karl-Heinz Janßen, "Staatstheaterstreich in Stuttgart: In der Politik ein Konservativer," *Die Zeit,* 26 May, 1970, p. 9. Hochhuth seems to confirm this himself (K, 236).

2. For more information on Hochhuth's close relationship with L. L. Matthias see his *Nekrolog,* written after the latter's suicide in 1970, *Die Hebamme,* pp. 461–82. Works by Matthias that may have influenced Hochhuth: Leo L. Matthias, *Es hing an einem Faden: Meine Jahre in*

*Lateinamerika und in Europa* (Reinbek, 1970); *Die Kehrseite der USA* (Reinbek, 1971).

3. Although Hochhuth makes no specific reference here, he is undoubtedly referring to Edward Luttwak, *Coup d'état: a practical handbook* (London, 1968).

4. The original quotation is difficult to translate; it refers specifically to the reaction to Hochhuth's *Soldiers* in New York. "Wieder einmal hatte sich erwiesen, daß der Schriftsteller ein risikolos zu integrierender Unterhaltungs-Clown der Gesellschaft ist, garantiert ungefährlich wie eine Anti-Kriegs Demonstration, nützlich als Nachweis gegenüber dem Anstand, daß die Freiheit des Wortes gewährleistet ist... (K, 236–37).

5. The similarity in choice of words is striking; in the "Historische Streiflichter" Hochhuth had stated: "Die Wirklichkeit blieb stets respektiert, sie wurde aber entschlackt" (St, 229). "Reality was respected throughout, but much of its slag had to be removed" (De, 287).

6. Hochhuth indicates that this quotation comes from a letter, but as usual he gives no specific reference. In German it reads: "'Der Neuere schlägt sich mühselig und ängstlich mit Zufälligkeiten und Nebendingen herum, und über dem Bestreben, der Wirklichkeit recht nahe zu kommen, beladet er sich mit dem Leeren und Unbedeutenden, und darüber läuft er Gefahr, die tiefliegende Wahrheit zu verlieren, worin eigentlich alles Poetische liegt. Er möchte gern einen wirklichen Fall vollkommen nachahmen und bedenkt nicht, daß eine poetische Darstellung mit der Wirklichkeit eben darum, weil sie absolut wahr ist, niemals koinzidieren kann...'" (G, 21).

7. This transformation took place over a period of time and culminated in the 1965 programmatic statement, "Zehn Arbeitspunkte eines Autors in einer geteilten Welt." See *Materialien zu Peter Weiss Marat/Sade,* edition suhrkamp 232 (Frankfurt am Main, 1967), pp. 114–119.

8. Weiss, "Das Material und die Modelle," p. 469.

9. This shared position can be contrasted with the approach advocated by Hans Magnus Enzensberger in the introduction to *Das Verhör von Habana* (Frankfurt, 1970), pp. 52–54, where Enzensberger specifically calls for "recreation, reproduction" of the event.

10. Weiss, "Das Material und die Modelle," pp. 467–68.

11. *Ibid.,* p. 465.

12. *Ibid.,* p. 469.

13. Janßen, "In der Politik ein Konservativer," p. 10.

14. The figure of Nicolson, although not based on any historical model, does resemble in some of these traits Senator John Kennedy. Even Nicolson's wife is compared to Jacqueline Kennedy (G, 41).

15. Weisstein, p. 103. The original source is cited as *Neue Zürcher Zeitung,* March 22 and 23, 1945.

16. Hochhuth's chauvinist attitude toward women is quite evident in all three tragedies. Particularly revealing is the following description of Helga in *The Deputy:* "She is well-endowed with the specifically feminine abilities to adopt opinions of those who impress her, and to see nothing that might disturb her. Like all distinctly feminine traits, those qualities are so innate in her that she would find even Auschwitz 'all right,' if she even gave it any thought. Of course she never does. Hence, she is a particularly tempting opiate for men here, who sometimes see ghosts at night" (De, 228–30). Helen, the only female character in *Soldiers,* is not taken much more seriously. She is depicted primarily in her role as secretary to the prime minister, and she is also used to provide some "love interest."

17. It has been suggested that Professor Wiener's position — a conservative one — is more truly that of Hochhuth, but this ignores the political essays, which suggest a closer identification between the author and his tragic hero. See Janßen, "In der Politik ein Konservativer," p. 10.

18. "So kommt die Nemesis über Amerika.../ weil dort, wo wir bauten und säten/ die Erde weich ist vom Blut der Ermordeten,/ denen wir das Land raubten und die Herden —/ ohne Blick dafür, ohne Dank,/ daß dieser unverbrauchteste, hoffnungsvollste Acker,/ den je Gott Einwanderern geschenkt hat —/ Frucht genug hatte und Tiere und Raum,/ den neuen Siedlern mit jenen Brot und Gold zu spenden,/ die auf dieser Erde geboren waren" (G, 109).

19. Hellmuth Karasek, "Staatstheaterstreich in Stuttgart: In der Dramaturgie ein Klassizist," *Die Zeit,* 26 May 1970, p. 10.

20. *Ibid.*

21. "Hochhuths Geschichts-Phantasie — und das ist eine unvermeidliche Konsequenz aus ihrer hysterischen und faschistischen Vereinfachungssucht — realisiert sich dramatisch und dramaturgisch in — Kolportage." Henning Rischbieter, "Rolf Hochhuth 'Guerillas' am Staatstheater Stuttgart," *Theater heute,* June 1970, pp. 14–15. See also *Krieg und Klassenkrieg,* p. 246, for remarks of this nature by Hans Heinz Holz of the *Frankfurter Rundschau,* quoted by Hochhuth. According to Holz, Hochhuth's concept of history and drama was the same as that of the president of Hitler's *Reichsschrifttumskammer* (academy of writers).

22. Karasek, p. 10.

23. *Ibid.*

## Chapter Six

1. Janßen, "Der Pessimist im Dorfkrug," p. 4.

2. Hochhuth uses the word "pessimism" to refer to Ludwig Marcuse's philosophy in the section subtitled "Für die 'unverlorenen Illusionen' Ludwig Marcuses," (H, 359–60), but in describing his own position he prefers the term *sachlich* (objective [H, 388]). Hochhuth does not cite any

specific works by Ludwig Marcuse in the essay, but he may have been influenced by the following: Ludwig Marcuse, *Argumente und Rezepte: ein Wörterbuch für Zeitgenossen* (Munich, 1967); *Mein zwanzigstes Jahrhundert, auf dem Weg zu einer Autobiographie* (Munich, 1960); *Obszön, Geschichte einer Entrüstung* (Munich, 1962); *Die Philosophie des Glücks von Hiob bis Freud* (Meisenheim am Glan, 1949; and Zürich, 1972); *Plato und Dionys: Geschichte einer Demokratie und einer Diktatur* (Berlin, 1968). The last of these books is available in translation: *Plato und Dionysius: A double biography,* trans. Joel Ames (New York, 1947). Hochhuth invariably refers to philosophers and historians without noting specific works: this is true here of Herbert Marcuse, Jakob Burckhardt, and Karl Jaspers as well as Ludwig Marcuse.

3. Despite Hochhuth's differences with the German student movement, he specifically advocates the long march through the institutions outlined by Rudi Dutschke, but this otherwise "realistic" revolution should also include parliament, according to Hochhuth. ("Ein Postulat: Dutschkes 'langer Marsch' muß *auch* durch das Parlament gehen," [H, 372–74]).

4. Peter Weiss, "Gespräch über Dante," in *Rapporte,* edition suhrkamp, 444 (Frankfurt am Main, 1968), pp. 135–50. For Weiss the discovery of a "heiles Weltbild" implies a rejection of the absurd: "Heute wird oft eine Ausweglosigkeit dargestellt und die unmöglichen Bemühungen, aus der Ausweglosigkeit herauszukommen. In Ermangelung von danteschen Lösungen werden nur Handlungen gefunden, die absurd erscheinen" ("Today one often portrays a dead end and the impossible efforts to get out of that dead end. For lack of a solution like Dante, we create plots which appear absurd"), pp. 147–48.

5. Albert Camus, *The Myth of Sisyphus and other essays,* trans. Justin O'Brien (New York, 1959), pp. 2–102.

6. Strothmann, p. 2.

7. Rolf Hochhuth, "Zigarillos," *der Zeit* übermittelt von Karl Hoche, *Die Zeit,* 29 September 1970, p. 10.

8. Fritzdieter Gerhards, "'Am liebsten schriebe ich nur Komödien': Der Essener Dramaturg sprach mit Rolf Hochhuth," *Die Deutsche Bühne,* February 1974, p. 16.

9. Hochhuth cites no source for the Stendhal quote other than the date 13 September 1817. The epilogue, entitled "Ein Blick auf Wörter: zum Beispiel 'Endlösung' und 'wohnungsunwürdig'" ("A consideration of words: for example 'final solution' and 'not worthy of housing'"), investigates the link between our use of language and our understanding of reality. Hochhuth speculates whether the use of bureaucratic euphemisms and jargon to describe situations of abject misery in fact contributes to them (H, 297).

10. The rather broad farce of Hochhuth's scene contrasts with the verbal subtlety of Kleist's famous comedy, but nevertheless a similarity in situation justifies a brief comparison. Although Bläbberberg is not on trial here, he does try to use his role as judge to cover up his illegal dealings; like Dorfrichter Adam he is continually stalling and tries to move away from the central issue.

11. Even such a remark reveals Hochhuth's attitude toward women. He seems to find the idea of an elderly lady undertaking such a revolutionary act in itself humorous, and his audiences may agree. According to this view, the natural thing would be for the men to take the lead, but here the sex-stereotyped roles are comically reversed. Numerous jokes at the expense of women are made throughout the play (H, 117, for example).

12. Hellmuth Karasek, "In Hochhuths Kreißsaal: 'Die Hebamme' — die erste Komödie des 'Stellvertreter' Autors," *Die Zeit,* 16 May 1972, p. 11. It can be said in Hochhuth's defense that *Die Hebamme* has considerable "depth" when compared to a comedy like Carl Zuckmayer's *Der fröhliche Weinberg,* which uses similar techniques of dialect humor and stereotyping of characters.

13. Renate Voss, "Leserbriefe: Wieso schreibt Hochhuth aus provinzieller Rechthaberei?" *Die Zeit,* 13 June 1972, p. 22.

14. Peter Iden, "In Hochhuths Kreißsaal: Die Kasseler Aufführung," *Die Zeit,* 16 May 1972, p. 12.

15. Dieter Bachmann, "In Hochhuths Kreißsaal: Die Zürcher Aufführung," *Die Zeit,* 16 May 1972, p. 12.

16. Hayo Matthiesen, "Das Elend, Hochhuth und die CDU," *Die Zeit,* 31 August 1971, p. 10.

17. Gerhards, p. 16.

18. Karasek, "In Hochhuths Kreißsaal: 'Die Hebamme'...," p. 11.

19. "Laughter in the Slums," *Newsweek,* 22 May 1972, p. 106. The *Werkstatistik des Deutschen Bühnenvereins* (statistics for all German-speaking theaters in the Federal Republic, Switzerland, and Austria) for *Die Hebamme* are as follows: 1971-1972, 110 performances, 7 productions, 58,025 attendance; 1972-73, 417 performances, 20 productions, 241, 447 attendance; 1973-1974, 103 performances, 5 productions, 46,716 attendance. These statistics are recorded in *Die Deutsche Bühne,* December 1972, 1973, and 1974, p. 26. See also the positive review of the Munich production, Henry Popkin, "Hochhuth Comedy?" *Christian Science Monitor,* 10 July 1972, p. 12.

20. Gerhards, p. 16.

21. *Ibid.*

22. *Ibid.* Hochhuth seems to contradict himself in this interview. While specifically rejecting the terms "documentary drama" and "political theater," ("'Die Hebamme' sowohl wie 'Der Stellvertreter' sind in keinem höheren Maße dokumentarisch als zum Beispiel 'Der Hauptmann von

Köpenick', und sie sind nicht politischer als, sagen wir, 'Ein Bruderzwist in Habsburg,''') he nevertheless explains that his objective is to try to avoid the problem that "politisches Theater leicht Lehrtheater wird."

23. Examples of the cliché-ridden language in *Lysistrate* are the following: KONSTANTINOS: "Bildung hilft zur Klugheit nichts! (L, 31); KOUMANTAROS: "Frauen und Straßenbahnen soll man nie nachlaufen: kommen immer neue." (L, 32); KONSTANTINOS: "Hetz nicht: Wasser, das man noch trinken muß, wühlt man nicht auf" (L, 32).

24. An example of Hochhuth's sexual humor is that the minister's villa is called "Coitusculum." He calls, on the one hand, for naturalness, an acceptance of nudity in the bath scenes, while making remarks like the following to describe the appearance of the maid after making love: "die Bluse hat sie anbehalten — von ihrer nackten Brust genau soviel wie die Sittenpolizei des Zeitalters (und die Qualität des Busens) vorzuzeigen gestatten" (L, 16). Hochhuth also resorts to ellipsis whenever it comes to a real obscenity, for example, when the minister recites the following ditty: "Siesta-Mensch und Tiere schlafen, das Alter hält ein Nickerchen, die Jugend macht ein F...ckerchen" (L, 73). For an interesting study of the role of obscenity in Aristophanes see Thalien M. de Wit-Tak, *Lysistrata: Vrede, Vrouw en Obsceniteit bij Aristophanes* (Groningen, 1967), pp. 125–33.

25. Alexis Solomos, *The Living Aristophanes* (Ann Arbor, 1974), pp. 19 and 61.

26. *Ibid.,* p. 185.

27. See Johann Jakob Bachofen, *Mutterrecht und Urreligion,* ed. Rudolf Marx (Stuttgart, 1954), or *Myth, Religion and Mother Right,* trans. Ralph Manheim (Princeton, N.J., 1967). Also Germaine Greer, *The Female Eunuch* (New York, 1970).

28. See *Werkstatistik des Deutschen Bühnenvereins* in *Die Deutsche Bühne,* December 1974, p. 26.

29. Hellmuth Karasek, "Rolf Hochhuths siebter Sinn," *Der Spiegel,* 25 February 1974, p. 114. For another rare critique of the play see Ulrich Schreiber, "Die neueste Lysistrata: Rolf Hochhuth und das politische Theater," *Merkur,* 28 (1974), 488–90.

30. "Zur Erstaufführung gelangt 'Lysistrate und die Nato' von Rolf Hochhuth," *Theater der Zeit,* March, 1975, p. 13.

31. Dürrenmatt, p. 31.

32. *Ibid.,* p. 29.

33. See my comments, Chapter 1, p. 17. Walter Hinck (p. 83) agrees: "So erweist sich die Rückwendung zu Schiller als eine Gegenwendung gegen Dürrenmatt."

34. Gerhards, p. 16: "...daß politisches Theater leicht Lehrtheater wird und daß die Menschen es heute endlich leid sind, sich von der Bühne herab belehren zu lassen. Wenn das doch geschehen soll, und das soll dur-

chaus geschehen in meinen Komödien, dann muß es lachend geschehen. Ich bin der Meinung, Sozialpolitik ist ein viel zu ernstes Anliegen, als daß man sie ohne Humor betreiben könnte.''

35. Dürrenmatt, p. 33. In *21 Punkte zu den Physikern,* Dürrenmatt reiterated this point: ''Die Dramatik kann den Zuschauer überlisten, sich der Wirklichkeit auszusetzen, aber nicht zwingen, ihr standzuhalten oder sie gar zu bewältigen.'' In *Theaterschriften und Reden I* (Zürich, 1966), p. 194. Although Dürrenmatt thinks that the comedy can lure the audience into a confrontation with reality, unlike Hochhuth, he clearly draws the line there.

36. Dürrenmatt, *Problems of the Theatre,* p. 36. In *21 Punkte zu den Physikern,* Dürrenmatt also makes it clear that his starting point is a story, a happening, not a thesis. This also distinguishes him from Hochhuth. It cannot be my task here to discuss Dürrenmatt's essays on the theater in detail. I only wish to show the way in which Hochhuth's new position was close to Dürrenmatt's in *Theaterprobleme.* For further study of Dürrenmatt's dramaturgy and drama theory see also: Friedrich Dürrenmatt, *Theaterschriften und Reden II, Dramaturgisches und Kritisches* (Zurich, 1972); and ''Sätze über das Theater,'' in *Text und Kritik,* 50/51 (May 1976), 1-17.

37. Dürrenmatt, *Problems of the Theatre,* p. 32.

38. *Ibid.,* pp. 17 and 121.

39. *Ibid.,* p. 23. In *21 Punkte zu den Physikern,* Dürrenmatt emphasizes the importance of a dramatic plot (*Handlung*) and of chance (*Zufall*), *Theaterschriften und Reden I,* p. 193. In *Theaterprobleme* he talks only of ''some special tension or special condition'' without which there can be no dialogue.

40. Dürrenmatt, *Problems of the Theatre,* p. 31. It is at this point that Dürrenmatt introduces the idea of the Grotesque. ''Guilt can exist only as a personal achievement, as a religious deed.... Our world has led to the grotesque as well as to the atom bomb, and so it is a world like that of Hieronymus Bosch whose apocalyptic paintings are also grotesque.'' Hochhuth, on the other hand, stops just short of the grotesque, even in his comedies, because he still believes in individual guilt and responsibility.

41. *Ibid.,* p. 32.

42. Camus, p. 90. ''Sisyphus, proletarian of the gods, powerless and rebellious, knows the whole extent of his wretched condition.... The lucidity that was to constitute his torture at the same time crowns his victory.''

43. Dürrenmatt, *Problems of the Theatre,* p. 36.

44. Camus, p. 11.

45. *Ibid.,* p. 40.

46. *Ibid.,* p. 77. On the subject of guilt and responsibility Camus says: ''there may be responsible persons, but there are no guilty ones....'' p. 50.

47. Martin Esslin, *The Theatre of the Absurd* (New York, 1961), pp. xx.

48. *Ibid.,* p. 294.

49. Hochhuth had apparently accepted language as a vehicle of communication in his tragedies, but not without questioning it. For an analysis of *Soldiers* as a way of revealing the repressive nature of authoritarian language see Jack D. Zipes, "The Aesthetic Dimensions of the German Documentary Drama," *German Life and Letters,* XXIV (1970-71), 346-58. The essay on words at the conclusion of *Die Hebamme* indicates a heightened awareness of language as jargon and cliché. The use of cliché expressions and euphemisms in both comedies may also indicate a greater appreciation by Hochhuth of the position of the Absurd theater that language has been diverted from the expression of real content to the concealment of the truth. But all of Hochhuth's plays lack the radical probing of the limits of language that characterizes the Theater of the Absurd.

50. Esslin, *The Theater of the Absurd,* p. 294.

## Chapter Seven

1. Gerhards, p. 16.

2. Even the existence of *Juristen* is not well documented. Other than the Gerhards interview cited above, it is mentioned only in Edgar Neis *Rolf Hochhuth Der Stellvertreter — Soldaten,* Königs Erläuterungen 166/67 (Hollfeld/Obfr., n.d.), p. 45, but no publication information is given, just the date 1974. It does not appear in any German bibliography for the years 1970-1976. Rowohlt Verlag reported to me as of February 1977 that no finished manuscript exists, since Hochhuth had postponed the plan for *Juristen.* But he intends to return to it shortly, after completing a book on the fate of the German battleship, *Tirpitz.*

3. Testimonials for Pope John XXIII, Otto Flake, Erwin Piscator, and L. L. Matthias were included in *Die Hebamme* collection (H, 439-82). The last of these obituaries is particularly interesting for *Tod eines Jägers* because Matthias committed suicide at the age of seventy-seven. He was unable to go on living without his wife, particularly since blindness limited his ability to read and write. Hochhuth had received advice from Matthias for both *Guerillas* and *Die Hebamme.* He was particularly moved by this man's suicide, having spoken to him only hours before his death, and the testimonial reflects on the reasons for Matthias' action.

4. Rolf Hochhuth, *Die Berliner Antigone: Novelle* (Reinbek, 1975). See review of a dramatic reading of the novella at the Vienna Volkstheater by Kurt Kahl in *Theater heute,* March, 1966, pp. 44-45.

5. Camus, p. 3.

6. *Ibid.,* p. v.

7. *Ibid.,* p. 4.

8. See Gottfried Benn, "Altern als Problem für Künstler," ("Aging as a Problem for Artists") in *Gesammelte Werke* (Wiesbaden, 1962), I, 552–82.

9. Hemingway was known for his *machismo*. Hochhuth was therefore able to have his Hemingway figure repeat views on women that the author had already expressed in "Frauen und Mütter...." The following example on the copying nature of women is an echo of that essay: "But biographies will reveal that even though women are generally more intelligent than their husbands — and often more energetic as well — they still are always copies of their men. Even in a group they emancipate themselves by trying to become judges and pastors too, instead of sending our whole silly male world straight to hell and establishing a female world ... women still copy 'their' concepts from their oppressors" (T, 74).

10. See Günther Rühle, "Zehn Jahre Drama, Zehn Jahre Theater," *Theater 1975,* Sonderheft of *Theater heute,* pp. 107–18. He points out that *Sterbevorgänge* (the process of dying) became a popular theme in plays after 1970, naming Dorst's *Eiszeit,* Henkel's *Olaf und Albert,* and Mühl's *Rheinpromenade,* as well as Salvatore's *Büchners Tod,* which deals specifically with the author Georg Büchner. But as early as 1971 Peter Weiss had written a play, *Hölderlin* (Frankfurt am Main, 1971), about an author who had eventually gone insane.

11. Tankred Dorst, *Eiszeit,* edition suhrkamp, 610 (Frankfurt am Main, 1973), p. 120.

12. *Ibid.,* p. 109.

13. See A. E. Hotchner, *Papa Hemingway: A Personal Memoir* (New York, 1966, c. 1955); and Carlos Baker, *Ernest Hemingway: A Life Story* (London, 1969). Hochhuth seems to have drawn particularly on the final chapters of the Baker bibliography, for example the incident when Hemingway kissed the hem of the Cuban flag (p. 648) or the detail concerning his invitation to John Kennedy's inauguration (p. 656), as well as the specifics of his delusions concerning an investigation by the FBI (p. 653). Hochhuth was also familiar with the following biography, although it was less important as a source since it deals with Hemingway's early years: Leicester Hemingway, *My Brother, Ernest Hemingway* (New York, 1961).

14. Gregory H. Hemingway, M.D., *Papa: A Personal Memoir* (Boston, 1976). See *Tod eines Jägers,* p. 33, for an indication that Hochhuth knew this memoir.

15. *Ibid.,* p. 16.

16. "... denn Bücher, wenn sie Kriege wie Ausflüge schildern, halten länger als die ehrlichen. Hat doch die Wahrheit einen sehr geringen Stellenwert im Gedächtnis der Menschheit —" (T, 72).

17. "Die Ohnmacht des Einzelnen vor dem Elend der meisten, die hab'
ich ausgesprochen, ja. Aber nie: daß nur die Gemeinschaft da helfen kann,
die neue, die linke, denn die alte, die rechte hatte vierhundert Jahre Zeit —
und half nicht" (T, 103).

18. Leicester Hemingway, p. 203.

19. *Ibid.,* p. 82.

20. "— hat nie den Hinterhalt von Resignation und Trauer selber zu
fürchten gehabt, dem ich jede lebensbejahende Zeile ablisten mußte..."
(T, 100).

21. Camus, p. v.

22. At the time of this writing productions have been announced for
*Tod eines Jägers* in Göttingen, Vienna, Rostock and during the Salzberg
Festival in 1977. In the latter Curd Jürgens and Bernhard Wicki are to
share the role. See *Der Spiegel,* 25 October 1976, p. 20.

## *Chapter Eight*

1. Piscator, "Introduction to *The Deputy,*" in *Storm,* p. 15.

2. "Der Schriftsteller ist die Machtlosigkeit in Person: Nicht, was er
schreibt, sondern wo er es unterbringt, entscheidet darüber, ob er gehört
wird" (K, 69).

3. Allan Lewis, *Ionesco.* Twaynes World Authors Series 239 (New
York, 1972), p. 106.

4. Egon Schwarz, "Rolf Hochhuth's 'The Representative,'" *Germanic Review,* XXXIX (1964), 230.

5. Esslin, *The Theatre of the Absurd,* p. xvii.

6. These categories are based in part on those suggested as generally
valid criteria by Esslin in *The Theatre of the Absurd,* p. 309.

7. An example of how one play by Hochhuth can be evaluated simply
in terms of its major productions is given by Sidney F. Parham, "Editing
Hochhuth for the Stage: A Look at the Major Productions of *The
Deputy,*" *Educational theatre journal,* 28 (1976), 347–53.

8. Taëni, p. 35. "Das Angliegen des Polemikers und epischen Dichters:
'Die Welt muß verändert werden' — wird durch die (tragische) Einsicht,
daß die Welt in all ihrer Furchtbarkeit so ist, wie sie ist, nicht unbedingt
hinfällig."

9. Rühle, "Zehn Jahre Drama, zehn Jahre Theater," p. 118.

# Selected Bibliography

PRIMARY SOURCES

1. German editions
*Die Berliner Antigone.* Prosa und Verse. rororo, 1842. Reinbek bei Hamburg: Rowohlt, 1975. Includes the novella and poems, with an introduction by Nino Erné.
*Die Berliner Antigone.* Eine Erzählung. Gesprochen von Hannes Messemer. Dialogszene aus "Der Stellvertreter," Gesprochen von Hannes Messemer und Michael Degen. Hamburg: Deutsche Grammophon Gesellschaft Literatur Archiv, 1966. Available as a recording with a scene from "Der Stellvertreter."
*Dramen: Der Stellvertreter, Soldaten, Guerillas.* Sonderausgabe. Reinbek: Rowohlt, 1972. A special edition. In addition to the three tragedies it includes essays by Clive Barnes, Jack Kroll, Golo Mann, Ludwig Marcuse, Walter Muschg, Erwin Piscator, and H. C. N. Williams, provost of Coventry Cathedral.
*Guerillas.* Tragödie in 5 Akten. Reinbek: Rowohlt, 1970. Includes an important introduction by the author explaining his dramaturgy. Also available as rororo-theater, 1588. Reinbek: Rowohlt, 1973.
*Die Hebamme — Komödie — Erzählungen, Gedichte, Essays.* Die Bücher der Neunzehn, 203. Reinbek: Rowohlt, 1971. In addition to the comedy *Die Hebamme,* this collection includes: narrative prose, "Resignation oder die Geschichte einer Ehe" (1959), *Die Berliner Antigone* (1961), "L'Impromptu de Madame Tussaud" (1968), "Anekdote" (1970); poetry under the headings "Blätter aus einem Geschichtsatlas," "Deutschland braucht Bayern," "Privatissime," and "Reisenotizen"; essays, "Soll das Theater die heutige Welt darstellen?" (1963), "Appell an Verteidigungsminister Schmidt" (1970), "Unsere 'abgeschriebenen' Schriftsteller in der Bundesrepublik" (1970), "Hat die Revolution in der Bundesrepublik eine Chance?" (1968), "Der alte Mythos vom 'neuen' Menschen" (1969–71); and testimonials for Pope John XXIII, Otto Flake, Erwin Piscator, and L. L. Matthias.
*Die Hebamme — Komödie.* rororo-theater, 1670. Reinbek: Rowohlt, 1973.

165

*Die Hebamme: Komödie.* Berlin: Verlag Volk und Welt, 1973. This edition of the comedy published in the German Democratic Republic has a commentary by Heinz Plavius.

*Krieg und Klassenkrieg.* Studien. rororo, 1455. Reinbek: Rowohlt, 1971. Includes an introduction by Fritz J. Raddatz, "Die Verantwortung des Intellektuellen: Zum Impetus der Arbeiten Rolf Hochhuths," and the following essays, articles, and letters by the author: "Der Klassenkampf ist nicht zu Ende," "Die Diskussion des Aufrufs zum Klassenkampf," "Brief an einen Kommunisten in der ČSSR," "Vom Soldaten zum Berufsverbrecher: Brief an den Bundespräsidenten und Schirmherrn des Deutschen Roten Kreuzes," "Die Sprache der Sozialdemokraten: Frankfurter Rede gegen die Notstandsgesetze am 28. Mai 1968," "Angst vor der 'Schutz'-Macht USA: Ein Rundblick nach der Ermordung Luther Kings und Robert Kennedys," "Zu 'Stellvertreter': Ein Gesamtbild gibt es nicht: Antwort an Wilhelm Alff," "Zu 'Soldaten': Gegen die *Neue Zürcher Zeitung*," "Zu 'Guerillas': Keine Revolution ohne Infiltration: Für Edward Luttwak gegen Hans Heinz Holz," "Zu 'Hebamme': Achthunderttausend Obdachlose in der Bundesrepublik."

*Lysistrate und die Nato.* Komödie. das neue buch, 46. Reinbek: Rowohlt, 1973. Includes a study by the author entitled "Frauen und Mütter, Bachofen und Germaine Greer."

*Soldaten: Nekrolog auf Genf.* Tragödie. Rowohlt Paperback, 59. Reinbek: Rowohlt, 1967. Also available as rororo-theater, 1323. Reinbek: Rowohlt, 1970. This latter edition includes a foreword by H. C. N. Williams and a commentary by Kathleen Tynan.

*Der Stellvertreter.* Schauspiel. Rowohlt Paperback, 20. Reinbek: Rowohlt, 1963. With a foreword by Erwin Piscator and "Historische Streiflichter."

*Der Stellvertreter.* Ein christliches Trauerspiel. rororo-theater, 997/998. Reinbek: Rowohlt, 1967. This edition, which has had five reprintings — most recently 1974 — includes essays by Sabine Lietzmann, Karl Jaspers, Walter Muschg, Erwin Piscator, and Golo Mann, as well as a variant of the fifth act.

*Der Stellvertreter.* Schauspiel. Berlin: Volk und Welt, 1965. This edition published in the German Democratic Republic has the Erwin Piscator introduction and documents collected by Klaus Drobisch.

*Tod eines Jägers.* das neue buch, 68. Reinbek: Rowohlt, 1976. There is no subtitle, but it is a monodrama.

*Zwischenspiel in Baden-Baden* Reinbek: Rowohlt, 1974. With illustrations by Werner Klemke. An expanded version of "Resignation oder die Geschichte einer Ehe," a short story that appeared in the *Hebamme* collection.

2. English editions

*The Deputy.* Trans. Richard and Clara Winston. New York: Grove Press, 1964. Includes a preface by Albert Schweitzer and "Sidelights on History" by the author. Also available with identical pagination as Evergreen Black Cat Paperback, B-154-T.

*The Representative.* Trans. Robert David MacDonald. London: Methuen, 1963. With a preface by Robert David MacDonald and "Historical Sidelights" by the author.

*Soldiers: An Obituary for Geneva.* Trans. Robert David MacDonald. New York: Grove Press, 1968. Also available with identical pagination as Evergreen Black Cat Paperback, B-200.

*Soldiers: An Obituary for Geneva.* Trans. Robert David MacDonald. London: André Deutsch, 1968. With an introduction by the provost of Coventry, H. C. N. Williams.


3. Works edited by Rolf Hochhuth

Busch, Wilhelm. *Sämtliche Werke und eine Auswahl der Skizzen und Gemälde.* 2 vols. Gütersloh: Bertelsmann Lesering, 1959–60. The two volume illustrated edition includes introductory remarks by Theodor Heuss taken from *Die großen Deutschen,* "Und die Moral von der Geschicht," and "Was beliebt ist auch erlaubt."

*Die großen Meister.* 2 vols. Cologne: Kiepenheuer and Witsch, 1966. A two volume selection by Hochhuth of European narrative prose of the twentieth century ("Europäische Erzähler des 20. Jahrhunderts").

*Liebe in unserer Zeit: 32 Erzählungen.* Hamburg: Rütten and Loening, 1961. With essays by Otto Flake and Martin Beheim-Schwarzbach.

Storm, Theodor. *Am grauen Meer: Gesammelte Werke.* Hamburg: Mosaik, 1962. A memorial edition for the seventy-fifth anniversary of Storm's death. Contains illustrations: paintings from the nineteenth and twentieth centuries, and drawings by Adolph Menzel.

Tellgmann, Oskar und Gustav. *Kaisers Zeiten: Bilder einer Epoche.* Ed. Rolf Hochhuth and Hans-Heinrich Koch. Munich: Herbig, 1973. Pictures from the archives of the court photographer brothers, Oskar and Gustav Tellgmann.


4. Articles, Essays, Letters, etc.

(This section is highly selective; it does not include any essays listed above under section 1. For interviews of Hochhuth see detailed references in the footnotes.)

"Das Absurde ist die Geschichte." *Theater 1963.* Sonderheft von *Theater heute,* pp. 73–74.

"Dieser Pole starb gelegen." *Der Spiegel,* 2 October 1967, pp. 133–34, 136–42.

"Er sah das Tragische nicht: Ein Brief über Bertolt Brecht." *Theater heute,* February 1967, p. 8.

"Man wird schon abgehärtet: Ein Brief darüber, wie die Theater mit dem Author umgehen." *Theater 1969.* Sonderheft von *Theater heute,* p. 10.

"Noch fünfzig Jahre schweigen." *Der Spiegel,* 9 October 1967, pp. 164, 166–67, 169–72, 174.

"Zigarillos," *Die Zeit,* 29 September 1970, p. 39.

"Zum Ruhme Sir Winstons." *Die Zeit,* 20 December 1968, pp. 27, 29. A book review of *Action this Day: Working with Churchill.* Ed. Sir John Wheeler-Bennett. London: Macmillan, 1968.

SECONDARY SOURCES

1. Books

MELCHINGER, SIEGFRIED. *Hochhuth.* Friedrichs Dramatiker des Welt-theaters, 44. Velber bei Hannover: Friedrich, 1967; rpt. 1972. This German monograph covers only the first two plays. Contains valuable information on individual productions with photographs. Chronology and bibliography.

NEIS, EDGAR. *Rolf Hochhuth: Der Stellvertreter — Soldaten.* Königs Erläuterungen, 166/167. Hollfeld: C. Bange, n.d. Intended for use by German pupils. Gives plot summaries, a small sample of criticism on the two plays, documentary material relevant to *Soldaten,* and a bibliography.

*The Storm over The Deputy.* Ed. Eric Bentley. New York: Grove Press, 1964. This valuable paperback includes a foreword by Bentley; the Piscator introduction; several important interviews; a wide range of criticism by journalists, theater critics, historians, and philosophers; and a lengthy bibliography compiled by David Beams.

*Der Streit um Hochhuths "Stellvertreter".* Ed. Reinhold Grimm, Willy Jäggi, and Hans Oesch. Kollektion Theater unserer Zeit, 5. Basle: Basilius Presse, 1963. A foreword by Jäggi. Divided into the following sections: "Wer ist Rolf Hochhuth?", "Das Stück und seine Auf-führung," "Wahrheit oder Fälschung?", "Durfte der Papst schweigen?", "Der Streit, Drama oder Pamphlet?". Includes a revealing portrait by a personal friend — the letter by Dieter Voll-precht; other letters to Hochhuth; Pope Paul VI's remarks and the author's reply; and the obituary for Pius XII written by Father Leiber.

*Summa iniuria oder Durfte der Papst schweigen? — Hochhuths "Stellver-treter" in der öffentlichen Kritik.* Ed. Fritz J. Raddatz. rororo-aktuell, 591. Reinbek: Rowohlt, 1963. Provides a wide selection of criticism with a foreword by Raddatz. In addition to letters to Hochhuth and his publisher, replies by the author to Wilhelm Alff, Msgr. Erich Klausener, and Albrecht von Kessel are also included.

TAËNI, RAINER. *Rolf Hochhuth.* Autorenbücher, 5. Munich: Verlag C. H. Beck and Verlag edition text + kritik, 1977. This monograph appeared in April 1977, too late to be taken into consideration in the text of this study. Taëni's book treats Hochhuth's life under the motto, "Bestechlichkeit durch Dankbarkeit," analyzes the major works and their effect, includes remarks by Ludwig Erhard as an appendix, and contains a short bibliography and chronology. Intended for a German audience already familiar with Hochhuth's major plays.

2. Essays in books on contemporary German literature

CARL, ROLF-PETER. "Dokumentarisches Theater." *Die deutsche Literatur der Gegenwart: Aspekte und Tendenzen.* Ed. Manfred Durzak, pp. 99–127. Stuttgart: Reclam, 1971. Excellent treatment of documentary drama as a dilemma — inability of the author to achieve synthesis of aesthetic and documentary elements. Discusses all three tragedies. Places Hochhuth against background of Realism debate of the 1930s. Good bibliography.

DEMETZ, PETER. "Rolf Hochhuth." In *Postwar German Literature: A Critical Introduction,* pp. 137–46. New York: Western, 1970. A portrait. Notes relationship between Hochhuth and Existentialist mood of the 1950s. Argues that *Soldiers* is superior to *The Deputy.*

HINCK, WALTER. "Von der Parabel zum Straßentheater: Notizen zum Drama der Gegenwart." *Poesie und Politik: Zur Situation der Literatur in Deutschland.* Ed. Wolfgang Kuttenkeuler, pp. 69–90. Stuttgart: Kohlhammer, 1973. Relates all contemporary German drama to Brecht tradition. Good comparison of Hochhuth with Frisch and Dürrenmatt. Distinguishes Hochhuth from documentary dramatists.

HOOVER, MARJORIE L. "Revolution und Ritual: Das deutsche Drama der sechziger Jahre. *Revolte und Experiment: Die Literatur der sechziger Jahre in Ost und West,* Poesie und Wissenschaft, 35. Ed. Wolfgang Paulsen, pp. 73–97. Heidelberg: Lothar Stiehm, 1972. Places Hochhuth in perspective of the drama of the 1960s. Comparison with Weiss, Dorst, Hacks, and others. Criticizes Hochhuth for a lack of style.

KESTING, MARIANNE. "Das deutsche Drama seit Ende des Weltkriegs." *Die deutsche Literatur der Gegenwart: Aspekte und Tendenzen.* Ed. Manfred Durzak, pp. 76–98. Stuttgart: Reclam, 1971. Discusses Hochhuth's contribution to German drama since the war. Treats him under the heading "Gesellschaftskritischer Realismus und politisches Dokumentartheater." Discusses only first two plays. Sees use of Schillerian model as presenting a dilemma.

————. "Rolf Hochhuth — Völkermord in Jamben." In *Panorama des Zeitgenössischen Theaters: 58 literarische Porträts.* 2nd ed., pp. 324–28. Munich: Piper, 1969. Covers only first two plays. A largely negative portrait. Misspells Hochhuth's name throughout.

KOEBNER, THOMAS. "Dramatik und Dramaturgie." *Tendenzen der deutschen Literatur seit 1945,* Kröners Taschenausgabe, 405. Ed. Thomas Koebner, pp. 365–66, 389, 438–42. Stuttgart: Kröner, 1971. Puts Hochhuth into total context of German drama since the war. Treats under heading of "documentary drama." A balanced approach.

KOPPERSCHMIDT, JOSEF. "Schuldhafte Schuldlosigkeit: Das Thema 'Schuld' in der modernen Literatur." *Der Mensch am Ende der Moral: Analysen an Beispielen neuerer Literatur.* Ed. Josef Blank, pp. 35–61. Düsseldorf: Patmos, 1971. Very good study of the problem of guilt. Compares *Der Stellvertreter* with Max Frisch's *Andorra,* Siegfried Lenz' *Zeit der Schuldlosen,* Friedrich Dürrenmatt's *Der Besuch der alten Dame,* and Peter Weiss' *Die Ermittlung.* Sees Hochhuth as the single exception for whom guilt and freedom of choice are still linked.

MENNEMEIER, FRANZ NORBERT. "Ein kleinbürgerlich-idealistischer Polemiker." *Modernes Deutsches Drama: Kritiken und Charakteristiken, II: 1933 bis zur Gegenwart,* pp. 252–62. Munich: Wilhelm Fink, 1975. A review of *Guerillas.* Interesting comparison with Camus. Argues that Hochhuth's dramatic form has been dictated by his political world view.

PARKES, STUART. "West German Drama since the War." *The German Theatre.* Ed. Ronald Hayman, pp. 129–47. London: Oswald Wolff, 1975. Compares Hochhuth to Weiss and Kipphardt in context of documentary drama. Interprets *Die Hebamme* as a rebirth of the *Volksstück.*

ZIPES, JACK D. "Das dokumentarische Drama." *Tendenzen der deutschen Literatur seit 1945.* Kröners Taschenausgabe, 405. Ed. Thomas Koebner, pp. 462–79. Stuttgart: Kröner, 1971. Treats Hochhuth in context of documentary drama. Considers only the first two plays. Interesting contrast to Max Frisch. Notes difficult reception in Germany.

3. Articles

(This section is highly selective; it does not include reviews of individual plays already referred to in the footnotes or those included in the books listed under section 1.)

ARENDT, HANNAH. "Der Stellvertreter in USA." *Neue deutsche Hefte,* 101 (September-October 1964), 11–123. Despite the title, it says little about *The Deputy* in the United States. Offers instead an examination of validity of Hochhuth's historical thesis. Outlines the replies of the church. Supports Hochhuth's thesis.

HILTON, IAN. "The Theatre of Fact in Germany." *Forum for Modern Language Studies,* IV (1968), 260-68. Treats Hochhuth in context of documentary drama. Adds comparison with lesser-known dramas: Felix Lützkendorf's *Dallas — 22. November* (1965) and Wolfgang Graetz' *Die Verschwörer* (1965). Notes dangers of documentary drama; argues need for universality.

KARESEK, HELLMUTH. "Die wahren Beweggründe: Dokumentartheater und die Folgen." *Akzente,* XIII (1966), 208-11. Notes the important influence of Hochhuth's first drama on all German theater. Sees as pendulum swing away from parable plays.

PERRY, R. C. "Historical Authenticity and Dramatic Form: Hochhuth's 'Der Stellvertreter' and Weiss's 'Die Ermittlung.'" *Modern Language Review,* LXIV (1969), 828-39. Good comparison of these two plays with emphasis on form — dictated by intent — and historical authenticity. Excellent discussion of Hochhuth's verse; comparison with Schiller's *Don Carlos.* Good discussion of Act V. Feels *Der Stellvertreter* has more limited polemical aim than *Die Ermittlung.*

ROUBICZEK, H. "'Der Stellvertreter' and its Critics." *German Life and Letters,* XVII (1963-64), 193-99. Emphasizes that most discussion has gone astray. Returns to the play itself, giving a largely positive critique. Criticism of MacDonald translation. Very good article for undergraduates.

SCHWARZ, EGON. "Rolf Hochhuth's 'The Representative.'" *Germanic Review,* XXXIX (1964), 211-30. Reviews other criticism of play. Discusses language, characters, and interrelation of form and content. Emphasizes epic nature of drama — not a real plot. A very balanced review; recommended highly for undergraduates.

TAËNI, RAINER. "'Der Stellvertreter': Episches Theater oder christliche Tragödie?" *Seminar,* II, no. 1 (Spring 1966), 15-35. Discusses Hochhuth's reintroduction of the tragic hero in relation to Brecht. Defines epic and tragic aspects by comparing it with Brecht's *Mutter Courage* and *Die heilige Johanna der Schlachthöfe.*

ZIPES, JACK D. "The Aesthetic Dimensions of the German Documentary Drama." *German Life and Letters,* XXIV (1970-71), 346-58. Analyzes documentary drama's attack on "ritual authoritarian language" by contrasting *Soldaten* with Günter Grass' *Die Plebejer proben den Aufstand* and Peter Weiss' *Gesang vom lusitanischen Popanz.*

———. "Documentary Drama in Germany: Mending the Circuit." *The Germanic Review,* XLII (1967), 49-62. Sees link between documentary drama of 1960s and Brecht-Piscator tradition. Treats only *Der Stellvertreter,* but praises its language and structure. Argues ultimate effect is as a work of art.

———. "Guilt Ridden Hochhuth." *New Theatre Magazine.* VIII, no. 2 (Spring 1968), 17-20. A review of *Soldiers.* Emphasizes American parallels. Notes influence of Jaspers' *The Question of Guilt (Die Schuldfrage,* 1946) on Hochhuth.

# Index

(The works of Hochhuth are listed under his name)

Absurd, Theater of the, 20-23, 46, 81-84, 118, 123-25, 141-42

Adorno, Theodor W., 18, 22, 62, 74, *81-85*, 97, 103, 118, 125

"Advance effect," 92, 98

Alff, Wilhelm, 46-47

Alienation, 22, 39-40, 64, 69; *See also Verfremdung*

Allegorical figure, 38, 41, 46, 60; *See also* Mystery plays

America, The United States of, 78-80, 85-87, 91, 94, 102, 115, 118, 133, 135-36, 141; President of, 63, 96

Arendt, Hannah: *Eichmann in Jerusalem*, 31

Aristophanes: *Lysistrata*, 111-15

Auschwitz, 19, 25, 27-32, 34, 36-37, 39-41, 46, 52, 61, 66, 127

Bachofen, Johann Jakob: *Mutterrecht und Urreligion*, 116

Baumgart, Reinhard, 62

Beckett, Samuel, 20, 82

Bell, Bishop of Chichester, 49, 52, 54-57, 59-60, 64

Benn, Gottfried, 128, 131

Böll, Heinrich, 76

Brandt, Willy, 76, 100, 108

Brecht, Bertolt,, 21-22, 42, 53, 64, 83-84, 96, 145; *Der aufhaltsame Aufstieg des Arturo Ui*, 22, 123

Brenner, Otto, 75, 77

British National Theatre, 51, 65

Burckhardt, Carl Jakob, 38, 101

Camus, Albert, 46, 103, 125, 127, 137; *The Myth of Sisyphus*, 122-24, 130-31

Capitalism, 62, 74-76, 78-79, 91

Chaplin, Charlie: *The Great Dictator* (film), 22, 123

Choice, freedom of, 17, 19, 36-37, 39, 54, 57, 80, 82, 104

Churchill, Winston, 23, 47-58, 60-61, 63, 65-66, 68-70, 92, 95

Comedy, 48, 70, 85, 96, 99, *100-25*, 145

Communism, 30, 62, 72, 77; *See also* Marxism

Concentration camps, 16, 19, 25, 27, 30, 37-38, 40-41, 66; *See also* Auschwitz

Coventry, cathedral of, 60, 64; provost of, 70

Dante, 102-103; *The Divine Comedy*, 33

*Diary of Anne Frank, The*, 28

Documentary drama, 20, 28, 52, 54, 58, 65, 67-68, 87, 89-90, 95, 111, 133, 143-44

Dorst, Tankred: *Eiszeit*, 131-32

Dresden, bombing of, 50, 58, 60-62; dead woman of, 61, 63, 127

Dürrenmatt, Friedrich, 17-18, 35, 118-24, 127; *Der Besuch der alten Dame*, 121; *Die Ehe des Herrn Mississippi*, 120; *Die Physiker*, 45; *Theaterprobleme*, 17, 118-20

Durzak, Manfred, 36

Eichmann, Adolf, 28, 31, 35, 39, 45

Enzensberger, Hans Magnus, 77, 156n9

Emergency laws, 76-77, 80, 154n7

Erhard, Ludwig, 76

Eschwege on the Werra, 15-17

Esslin, Martin, 18; *The Theatre of the Absurd*, 124, 141-42

*Everyman*, 54, 60, 69, 128, 152n20
"Extra-parliamentary" opposition, 76;
   *See also* Student movement

"Final solution," 25, 30, 35
Flake, Otto, 17
Freie Volksbühne (Berlin), 28, 52
Frisch, Max, 140; *Andorra*, 23, 28;
   "Über Zeitereignis und Dichtung,"
   92

Gerstein, Kurt, 25-27, 30-35, 37, 39-40
Greer, Germaine, 115-16
Grotesque, 35, 40, 46, 118, 121-22,
   161n40
Guevara, Che, 93, 95
Guilt, 23, 37, 39, 44, 60-62, 65-66, 121-
   25, 133, 143; *See also* Responsibility

Heinemann, Gustav, 50
Hemingway, Ernest, 124, 128, 130-34,
   137-38; *The Old Man and the Sea*,
   135; *To have and have not*, 136
Heuß, Theodor, 126-27
History. *See* Truth, historical
Hitler, Adolf, 17, 23, 25-26, 30, 46-47,
   49-50, 105, 114, 127
Hochhuth, Rolf: boyhood in wartime,
   15; divorce, 129; illness, 16; literary
   beginnings, 16-17; move to Basle, 74;
   university studies, 16; *Weltanschauung* of, 18, 20, 23, 36, 39, 76,
   84, 87, 97, 110, 123, 125; working as
   bookseller, 16
WORKS—DRAMA:
*Deputy, The* (*Der Stellvertreter*), 17, 19,
   23, *25-48*, 52-53, 56, 58-61, 63, 65,
   67-68, 73, 87-88, 95, 97-98, 111,
   118-19, 127, 140-45; "Historical
   Sidelights" to, 21, 26-27, 29, 44,
   46, 48, 72, 85
*Guerillas*, 79-80, *85-100*, 104-105, 108-
   109, 115, 121, 128, 141, 143
*Hebamme, Die* (*The Midwife*), 99-101,
   *104-11*, 114, 117, 119, 121, 126,
   141, 143
*Juristen*, 126-27

*Lysistrate und die Nato*, 99, 104, *111-
   21*, 126, 131, 143
*Soldiers* (*Soldaten*), 48-70, 72-73, 75,
   87, 89, 94-98, 104, 111, 127-28,
   134, 140, 143
*Tod eines Jägers* (*Death of a Hunter*),
   124, 127-28, *130-38*, 143, 144-45
"Zigarillos," 105
WORKS—POETRY:
   "Deutschland braucht Bayern"
   ("Germany Needs Bavaria), 105,
   126
WORKS—PROSE:
   "Alte Mythos vom 'neuen' Mens-
   chen, Der" ("The old myth of the
   'new' man"), 101, 107
   "Angst vor der 'Schutz'-Macht USA"
   ("Fear of the so-called protective
   power, USA"), 78-79, 85, 94, 115
   "Appell     an     Verteidigungsminister
   Schmidt" ("Appeal to defense
   minister Schmidt"), 100
*Berliner Antigone, Die*, 129
   "Frauen und Mütter, Bachofen und
   Germaine Greer" ("Women and
   Mothers, Bachofen and Germaine
   Greer"), 115-17, 131
   "Hat die Revolution in der Bundesre-
   publik eine Chance?" ("Does
   revolution have a chance in the
   Federal Republic?"), 77
   "Impromptu de Madame Tussaud," 70,
   151n9, 151-52n19
   "Keine Revolution ohne Infiltration"
   ("No revolution without infiltra-
   tion"), 79, 85, 87, 97
   "Klassenkampf ist nicht zu Ende, Der"
   ("The Class struggle is not yet
   over"), 71, 74-76, 80-81, 100
*Krieg und Klassenkrieg* (*War and Class
   War*), 51, 76, 83, 100
   "Soll das Theater die heutige Welt darstellen?" ("Should the theater pre-
   sent today's world?"), *17-22*, 81,
   84-85, 88, 123
   "Über Zuständigkeit von Nicht-Fachleuten" ("Concerning the compe-
   tence of Non-Specialists"), 71

"Unsere 'abgeschriebenen' Schrift-
stellar in der Bundesrepublik"
("Our writers in the Federal Republic who are 'written off'"),
100, 131
*Victoriastraße, Nr. 4*, 16-17
*Zwischenspiel in Baden-Baden* (*Inter-
mezzo in Baden-Baden*), 129-30

Ideology, 20, 22-23, 62, 64, 67, 72-74,
78, 80, 84, 89-90, 102
Individual, the, 18-19, 23, 26, 36, 47,
57, 62, 64, 75, 77, 79-84, 88, 102-103,
123, 125, 145
Ionesco, Eugène, 20, 141; *Rhinoceros*,
45
Irving, David, 51, 66, 69; *Accident*, 51,
*The Destruction of Dresden*, 49

Jaspers, Karl, 45, 101
Jews, 25-27, 29-35, 37, 40, 43-44, 46,
49, 56-57

Karasek, Hellmuth, 97-98, 108, 110, 117
Kennedy, John, 79, 95, 156n14, 163n13
Kennedy, Robert, 78-79, 95
King, Martin Luther, 78-79, 96
Kipphardt, Heinar, 68; *In der Sache J.
R. Oppenheimer*, 52, 67
Kleist, Heinrich von: *Der Zerbrochene
Krug*, 106-107
Kolbe, Father Maximilian, 27

Language, 21, 27, 40, 52, 68, 94, 125,
143-45, 158n9, 162n49
Ledig-Rowohlt, Heinrich-Maria, 28, 66,
70, 140; *See also* Rowohlt Verlag
Leiber, Father Robert, 43-44
Lenz, Reinhold Michael, 48, 150n2
Lessing, G.E., 66-67; *Nathan der
Weise*, 45
Lichtenberg, Provost Bernhard, 27
Lübke, Heinrich, 49-50, 59, 71-72, 75
Lukàcs, Georg, 18, 20, 81
Luttwak, Edward, 80, 86

Mann, Golo, 45

Mann, Thomas, 16-17, 67; *Betrachtun-
gungen eines Unpolitischen*, 17; *Bud-
denbrooks*, 17
Marcuse, Herbert, 101-104
Marcuse, Ludwig, 69, 101
Marx, Karl, 80, 102; Marxism, 67, 79-
80, 82, 90, 102-103
Matthias, Leo L., 86, 155-56n2, 162n3
Melville, Herman: *Moby Dick*, 135
Mengele, Joseph, 38
Mňačko, Ladislav, 103; *Verspätete Re-
portagen*, 72-73
Monologue, 38, 40-41, 61, 63, 94, 121,
127-30, 133-34, 137-38
Montini, G.B. Cardinal. *See* Paul VI,
Pope
Muschg, Walter, 45-46
Musil, Robert, 17
Mystery plays, 52, 54, 61, 65

Naturalistic, 20, 27, 40, 58-59, 88, 91,
94, 144
Nazis, 30-34, 46, 50, 73, 126
Niemöller, Martin, 25
Nixon, Richard, 95
*Notstandsgesetze. See* Emergency laws

Ortega y Gasset, 86, 88

Paul VI, Pope, 43-44
Personalization, of a conflict, 19, 26,
37, 51, 77, 82, 90, 147n9
Piscator, Erwin, 22, 28, 36-37, 41-42,
51-52, 61, 109, 139-40, 142
Poliakov, Leon: *Das Dritte Reich und
die Juden*, 25
Pius XII, Pope, 24-27, 29-39, 43-47, 49,
56, 58, 65, 92, 141

Realism, the problem of, 19-22, 38-41,
52, 59-60, 65, 82-84, 87-88, 94-95, 97,
105, 110, 114, 118, 120-21, 123, 135,
144-45
Red Cross, The, 50-51, 55, 62, 64
Responsibility, 18, 26, 34, 36, 39, 48,
62, 77, 109, 119, 121-25, 143; *See also*
Guilt

Rowohlt Verlag, 45; *See also* Ledig-Rowohlt
Russia, 15, 33, 35, 50-51, 55, 102, 115

Schiller, Friedrich, 17-22, 36, 67, 89, 98, 117-18; *Die Jungfrau von Orleans*, 67; *Maria Stuart*, 152n28; "Die Schaubühne als moralische Anstalt betrachtet," 23; "Über die tragische Kunst," 20-21; *Wallenstein*, 17, 19, 21
Schweikart, Hans, 52, 66, 68
Schweitzer, Albert, 45
Sikorski, General, 48, 51, 53-59, 65-66, 68-69, 95
Simon, John, 35-36
Sisyphus, 24, 84, 102-104, 107, 118, 122-25, 127, 131, 137, 145-46; *See also* Camus, Albert: *The Myth of Sisyphus*
Solomos, Alexis: *The Living Aristophanes*, 114-15
Sontag, Susan, 35-36
Soviet Union, The. *See* Russia
Spellmann, Francis Cardinal, 44, 95
Spengler, Oswald, 101
Springer, Axel, 74, 76
Stalin, Josef, 17, 51, 53, 56; Stalinism, 73
Star of David, 27, 32, 34
Student movement, 76-77, 87, 158n3
Surrealistic, 20, 41

Thompson, Carlos: *The Assassination of Winston Churchill*, 69-70

Tragedy, 18, 20-21, 29, 35, 41-42, 52-53, 65, 70, 75, 83, 85-86, 90, 97-98, 101, 103-104, 108, 117-18, 144-45; tragic hero, 17-18, 29-30, 42, 49, 53, 92, 94, 118-19, 121, 144; tragicomedy, 118-22
Truth, historical, 20-24, 28, 35-36, 46-47, 63-64, 66-67, 69, 73, 80, 85, 124, 137; poetic, 21, 66-67, 89, 143
Tynan, Kenneth, 65-66

USA. *See* America, The United States of
USSR. *See* Russia

Vatican, The, 25-26, 32, 38; *See also* Pius XII, Pope
*Verfrmedung*, 22, 39, 88, 96; *See also* Alienation
Vietnam, the war in, 50, 53, 60, 62, 64, 69, 79, 100

"War crimes," 34, 48, 50, 60
Weiss, Peter, 71-74, 90, 103; *Die Ermittlung*, 52, 67-68; *Gesang vom Lusitanischen Popanz*, 68; "Das Material und die Modelle," 21, 89-90; *Vietnam Diskurs*, 64
World War II, 15, 23, 48-49, 53, 60, 63, 70

Zuckmayer, Carl: *Der fröhliche Weinberg*, 159n12; *Des Teufels General*, 30